Casper 212:

Operation Just Cause
Panama

Pro-American/Anti-Noriega Guerilla Forces from the northern province of Chriqui, Panama and loyal to Doctor Hugo Spadafora

James Hoeber

NEWMAN SPRINGS PUBLISHING
320 Broad Street
Red Bank, NJ 07701

First originally published by Newman Springs Publishing 2020

ISBN 978-1-63692-136-5 (Paperback)
ISBN 978-1-63692-137-2 (Digital)

Printed in the United States of America

To those Americans and Panamanians, both soldiers and civilians, who fought with the American forces during "Operation Just Cause," and especially to the civilian Evergreen Helicopters Inc. personnel who were captured by hostile forces.

"OPERATION JUST CAUSE"

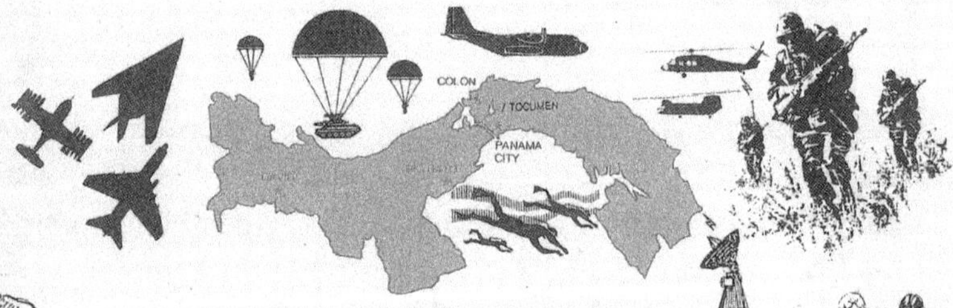

LET IT BE KNOWN THAT **Mr. James W. Hoeber, Evergreen/CASA Project, 61st MAG**

CONTRIBUTED UNSELFISHLY TO THE SUPPORT OF AMERICAN SOLDIERS, SAILORS, AIRMEN AND MARINES IN THEIR JOINT EFFORTS WITH THE PANAMANIAN PEOPLE TO ACHIEVE FREEDOM FROM TYRANNY AND TO GAIN SELF - DETERMINATION. DURING THIS HISTORIC PERIOD, THIS SELFLESS CONTRIBUTION TO THE RE-ESTABLISHMENT OF A DEMOCRATIC GOVERNMENT IN THE REPUBLIC OF PANAMA WAS IN KEEPING WITH THE HIGHEST IDEALS OF PUBLIC SERVICE AND A STEADFAST COMMITMENT TO DEMOCRACY AND FREEDOM.

CARL W. STINER
LTG, USA
Commanding General
Joint Task Force South

MAXWELL R. THURMAN
General, USA
Commander - In - Chief
Southern Command

The United States of America

Central Intelligence Agency

IN COMMEMORATION

During the hottest days of the Cold War, the aircrews and ground personnel of Civil Air Transport and Air America gave unwavering service to the United States of America in the worldwide battle against communist oppression. Over the course of four decades, the courage, dedication to duty, superior airmanship, and sacrifice of these individuals set standards against which all future covert air operations must be measured. From the mist-shrouded peaks of Tibet, to the black skies of China, to the steaming jungles of Southeast Asia, the legendary men and women of Civil Air Transport and Air America always gave full measure of themselves in the defense of freedom. They did so despite often outdated equipment, hazardous terrain, dangerous weather, enemy fire, and their own government bureaucracy. Their actions speak eloquently of their skill, bravery, loyalty, and faith in themselves, each other, and the United States of America.

George Tenet
Director of Central Intelligence
2 June 2001

This book contains some profanity. Although I refrain from the use of profane words or phrases in general, the appearance of certain words and phrases in this book are, I feel, necessary to give the reader a unique perspective of a particular situation.

Sometimes during adverse or intense conditions, the language of individuals will tend to degrade and not necessarily be the same language one might use at Thanksgiving dinner at Grandmother's house.

I hope that the use of strong words and phrases does not offend anyone. It has not been my intent to be vulgar in any sense, only to reflect accurately the demeanor of an individual or the intensity of a situation at a particular moment in time.

The Hangar

Jim Hoeber had no idea that crisp October morning that what would happen in the next few months would change his life forever. That morning, he had arrived at Potomac Field, a small airport that was nestled outside Washington, DC. It was small but the closest airfield to the district and was used by those who needed quick access in and out via their private plane. Jim had learned from one of the patrons of the field that just the night before, some unusual individuals had been by. They had inquired about his whereabouts. Although a common occurrence, these inquiries were always a prelude of things to come. Jim was thinking to himself, while busily working on a privately owned Cessna 152.

"Wonder what's up this time?" Jim mumbled under his breath. He was a seasoned veteran field rep. mechanic and flight engineer who had been newly assigned at Andrew Air Force Base. He had previously spent the last three years working the Mediterranean and North Africa out of Sigonella Naval Air Facility on the island of Sicily. Sigonella NAF was located about ten miles outside the city of Catania, a seaport south of the Straits of Messina. The navy used the base for an off-ship corrosion control and repaint depot, as well as for logistics support.

"Not too bad living back here in the real world again!" Jim said to himself. He stopped to think about what he had just said. "I wonder what those guys wanted? Awh, what difference does it make anyway? If they want me they know where to find me."

He thought it might have been some beer-drinking buddies wanting to go out and have a couple and reminisce about old times in South East Asia or maybe the "Gut" in Naples, Italy. Just about then, the wrench slipped off the bolt he was tightening on the rocker box cover, smashing his knuckles on the engine cowling.

"Goddamnit!" he shouted, as the blood dripped down his fingers.

"Man, I'm getting too old for this shit!" he yelled again, as if someone was around and would hear him, or even care. Having enough for the time being, he decided to head back to the hangar and get some first aid. Thinking to himself, if these guys come by this morning, it would definitely be "beer thirty," even if it wasn't even ten o'clock yet.

Early morning hours launching aircraft out at Andrews Air Force base for a nonappreciating Department of Defense contractor and then moonlighting out there in the boondocks was getting boring. Oh sure, the pay was good, but winter was coming up, and that meant less work, and the work you got was the pits. Outside or inside, rain or shine, hot or cold, it was all the same and getting old.

Just as Jim turned the corner at the side of the hangar, a big black Lincoln came screeching up to a stop just inches from him. Instinctively Jim flipped up the bird, throwing small splatters of blood across the windshield. Instantly, Bud Soucy jumped out, laughing so hard he was having trouble standing up.

"Bet I scared the crap out of you," he roared. Then upon seeing the red blood spots across his windshield like bullet holes, he backed off a little. "What's up?" Bud queried.

"You know, ever since I got into this business with you, it's been one thing after another," Jim fired back at Bud.

"Come on, let's go get some coffee and see what's on the agenda for today," he replied.

"Agenda!" Jim retorted "I've got your agenda hanging." He grabbed his crotch.

"Well, whatever!" Bud replied with a raised eyebrow as they both retired to the office that was situated in the back of the airplane crowded hangar.

"You know, some guys came by last night looking for you. I told Joe to let you know when you came by in this morning. Oh yeah, they left this number for you to call." Bud handed the piece of paper to Jim.

"Hey! This is a Washington number and inside the beltway too!"

"No shit, probably the IRS looking for you." Bud laughed.

Although the IRS could be looking into old records, it didn't bother Jim in the slightest, since the company had done all the tax reporting for its expatoriate employees.

"Oh, by the way, this one guy said something about Howard Air Force Base. Where in the hell is that anyway?" Bud asked.

Jumping up from the makeshift chair of old books and newspapers, Jim grabbed the phone, thinking if this is some kind of joke, he was going to beat the shit out of Bud. Slowly, as to not make a mistake, Jim dialed the number Bud had given him. After a couple of rings, a sweet nice young lady's voice announced, "State Department, Panama Desk."

"Hello! This is Hoeber, James W. Hoeber. I'm returning a message to call this morning."

"Just a moment. I'll connect you," she replied.

Bud looked puzzled. As Jim stood there, phone in hand, bleeding, waiting, he looked funny. Suddenly she came back on.

"I'm forwarding your call now," she said.

After a short pause, there came a familiar voice over the line.

"Hey, Jimbo, what's up? Came by yesterday, but they said you were out at Andrews. Glad you called, I was just stepping out for a while and—"

"Okay! Okay!" Jim cut in, "What's the deal this time?"

Jim knew something was up. Every time Colonel Moran looked him up, he got to take a trip to some interesting out-of-the-way place that most people can't pronounce, much less find on a map. Jim's contact with Colonel Moran went back, back about twenty years ago, to a time when both were stationed at Korat Air Base, Thailand. But the two of them had met there while on R & R from Da Nang Air Base, South Vietnam. Bud was working for IBM and on overseas assignment, taking care of some sort of information-gathering equipment they supplied the army with. While at Korat, Jim was temporarily transferred to Da Nang, where he again met up with Bud. Moran was a captain then and flew the helicopters that carried Bud's "boxes." Most of the time, it was military intel flights, but sometimes salvage was norm. Jim was the captain's crew chief and got to meet a lot of the tech reps that were working for the Department of Defense. The captain took a liking to Jim and Bud. In the subsequent years, their paths would cross many times, and now they were crossing again.

"Well, Dick, what's the news around the office?" queried Jim.

Jim knew that the colonel wasn't going to say anything right then, and even more so over the phone.

"Meet me at the yacht club around six, and I'll fill you in on the deal," responded Moran.

As so many times before, the ball was off and rolling—yacht club here, airstrip there, same old story. Help me out, and I'll help you out.

As Jim hung up, the numbness of the cold morning was wearing off, and the realization of what had happened earlier was fast becoming more painfully noticeable.

"Maybe you ought to put something on that," said Bud concernedly, pointing to Jim's still bleeding hand.

"Oh yeah, how about putting something on this!" said Jim sarcastically, again grabbing his crotch. Jim was still pissed off about almost getting run over, and he and Bud decided to call it a day and head into Clinton. There was a small bar in town that everybody from the air field hung out at. It was close to lunchtime, so off it was to town for a beer and burger.

C H A P T E R   2

Vanilla Extract

Sitting in the smoke-filled dimly lit yet comfortable bar, Jim's mind wandered back to a time when he had gotten to know Bud and then-captain Moran. That memorable and eventful occasion was as fresh now as it was then. He remembered getting up that morning—twelve o'clock midnight, to be more precise. He, as everyone else, was working a twelve and twelve for six and one. Twelve-hour shifts, six days on, and one off.

After a midnight chow of SOS, he entered the controlled area at the north perimeter gate. It was a short distance through the revetments to the open grassy area to where the helicopters were parked. Jim could still remember the stench of urine that permeated those revetments. Rounding the corner and then passing the racks of defoliant containers, he headed straight out across the ramp. Counting as he went, he was looking for spot 23 on the ready line.

"Twenty, twenty-one, twenty-two," he counted as he went along. Through the light fog, the NF2 LIGHT ALL made the CH-46 Chinook look like a giant armadillo. Walking up to it, he was the first one there. Jim picked up the forms and started flipping through the pages.

"Let's see what this bitch did last night," Jim mumbled. "Far out! No red X's, no damage, no leaks." Jim got the cover off and was over at the DASH power unit when the line truck drove up. The power unit's turbine engine was winding up, and he didn't see or hear the truck.

Bud, who was a civilian tech rep for the Department of Defense contractor that had equipment on these birds, walked up behind Jim, thinking that he was aware of his arrival.

"What's up, Chief?" Bud said, slapping Jim on the shoulder.

Instantly Jim covered ten feet of ground. You know, one second you're here, and *poof*, you're ten feet away. He could have been further, except that the headset and ground cord that was attached to the helo limited him to that ten feet or so.

Upon reaching that limit, it jerked him right down on the ground. Bud was doing everything he could to keep from laughing. Jim, to say the least, was ticked off. After giving Jim a hand up, Bud walked around the power unit and relieved himself, and that was that. Bud and Jim continued to shoot the shit till the aircrew approached the helo, Bud jumped up and offered his hand to his friend, Captain Moran.

"Captain, check it out. Jim Hoeber, fastest man on the ramp."

Captain Moran smiled. He didn't know what had happened.

"How's it hanging? Well, let's get this bitch up and see what it looks like!" the captain said.

As the whole ensemble mounted up and strapped in, Jim couldn't help but think that somehow he must have done something to someone somewhere to deserve this crap.

By now it was raining. Captain Moran poured to power to her and the familiar *whop, whop, whop* of the rotor blades got increasingly louder until the whole thing lifted off in a swirl of wind, water, and trash. After a few minutes of tension, things smoothed out, and everyone's asshole unpuckered.

About this time, Jim learned over to Bud and spoke. "See what it looks like?" he asked.

"Yeah," Bud replied, "seems there's a downed Huey that needs picking up."

"Do what?" exclaimed Jim.

"Piece of cake!" said Bud calmly. "Drop and hook. You know, sling it out. Nothing to it, right?"

"Nothing to it!" Jim mumbles under his breath. Last time it was nothing to it, he patched bullet holes for weeks.

The flight up-country was uneventful. Soon word came back that they were approaching the landing zone, and the helo started to descend. Once on the ground, they met up with a lieutenant whose men had secured the area that previous night. The aircraft that they were going to sling out had had engine trouble and was forced to do an emergency landing on the edge of a rice paddy outside a small village about half a klick from LZ.

Shortly, two Montagnards arrived and briefed the lieutenant and the captain. That there were not any hostiles in the area, but the situation could change at any moment. They had deployed a perimeter guard. Needless to say, expediency was of the necessity. Jim and his helper busily unloaded the tools they would need to remove the rotor blades. Since they were damaged beyond repair on the auto-rotation landing, all they needed was the chain saw. Jim readied the sling and cables, hook load with the sling, then radioed the aircrew to fly in, hover over the downed Huey, attach, and extract. If everything went off as planned, it would take less than thirty minutes.

After about an hour had passed, the radio suddenly came alive.

"Alpha One, this is Vanilla Extract. We're ready to bake a cake."

That was what the captain was waiting for. The helicopter shuddered as engine fired up, and soon the pilot, Captain Moran, Jim, Bud, and the grunts who came along for fire support were airborne. Once over the Huey, the personnel onboard were on their way back to the base. It was now a done deal.

That was easy, too easy, Jim thought to himself. *Maybe one day I'll do this for money.*

"What's so funny?" Bus asked. He had noticed Jim with a smile on his face.

Jim just kept smiling and didn't say a word.

C H A P T E R   3

Clinton, Maryland

As a couple of regular patrons entered through the portaled doors, a shot of cold air, cold northerly air, slapped Jim back to reality. Yes, this was Maryland, not Southeast Asia. Bud was just returning from the restroom. An old tear-jerking cowboy sang over the barroom jukebox speakers. Jolene was right in front of the table.

"I suppose you want a beer, and you want a scotch and water?" Jolene asked, first pointing to Jim and then Bud.

Bud answered with a quick comeback, "Does a bear shit in the woods or what?"

As she wiggled off, both Bud and Jim looked at her butt. After about four or five seconds, she disappeared behind the bar.

Bud and Jim just looked at each other. Without saying a word, they both new exactly what each other was thinking.

"Hey, Jim, you coming down to the yacht club tonight?" asked Bud. He had a certain kind of way he went about finding out things. First, asking the known, then popping up and hitting you with the real questions he wanted you to answer.

"Yeah, I think so. Ain't got nothing else to do," Jim answered. He looked around to see what happened to the waitress. "Where'd that wench go for the beer, DC?

"Maybe she's looking for a Panamanian beer," Bud slipped in.

"Yeah, I wish. An Atlas would do me good right now," Jim said as he opened and sipped an imaginary bottle of brew. Jim already knew what Bud was getting at. He wanted in on the deal.

If not actually participating in it, at least knowing all the details so he could at least add his point of view. Jim, still looking around for the chick with the drinks, looked at Bud, and after a moment or so says, "Tu habla espanol verdad? Este una condicion de trabajo aya. Tu sabes?"

Bud bolted back in his chair. "Don't start that Mexican shit with me. You know I don't speak spick."

Jim just laughed.

"What's so funny?" Bud asked.

Jim looked at Bud. "You got to speak Spanish if you're gonna hang with me, and by the way, *spick* is not a language, nor it is Mexican."

"What you trying to say? I'm fucked up or something?" he huffed.

Jim was getting agitated. "Speaking of fucked up, where in hell is that dingly broad? I swear that bitch ain't got one brain cell."

Suddenly in the front door walks Jolene. She walked right past the table where Bud and Jim were sitting. A smell of fresh perfume was in the air.

"I'll be right with you. I had to go home for a second," she calmly said.

Jim, thoroughly put out with her by now, jumped up and ran over to the bar. He ordered three beers and three scotch and waters. He returned and walked briskly back to the table where Bud was sitting and watching what was going on. Jim placed the drinks on the table, muttering something about how this was the correct amount of beverage that should have been consumed by now. It had been a full hour since first ordering. Bud and Jim sat there for the next hour or so discussing what needed to be done out at the airstrip. Time passed fast, and before long, it was time to leave and take care of the home front. Bud wasn't married anymore, so he just hung out at the Capital Yacht Club—that is, when he wasn't flying or out at the air field.

"Well, see ya tonight," Bud said as they both got up and headed for the door. Out in the parking lot, they went their own separate ways to attend to whatever needed to be done before it got too dark.

On the way back to the apartment, Jim was thinking about what was coming up and how he was going to deal with it. It was almost five thirty. He had a good head on but not so much that he was drunk. The apartment complex where he lives was right across from Andrews Air Force Base. This location made it convenient to commute to both his primary job at the base and his other job at Potomac Field, where he was employed as chief of maintenance. Pulling into the complex, he parked in his assigned parking slot. Jim's mind raced. He fantasized about the possibilities, possibilities that were not even close to being an eventual reality that he would experience. Once through the lower stairwell door, he smelled the different aromas of mouthwatering meals being prepared by persons unknown. This was typical every evening, as most of the apartment renters worked at Andrews and were just getting off now. They would soon be home and having a diner with their families. Jim's case wasn't any different.

Rosa was already home, so were the kids. Jim's wife had a day job working in the laundry room of a Motel 6 just two blocks from the apartments. She would go to work early in the morning and would be home before the children got home from school on the bus. Coming through the front door, Jim knew what was for dinner, arroz con pollo, or chicken rice, as it was called in English. This was Jim's favorite dish. Rosa knew how to make it especially well. Even when she was a little girl living in the remote highlands of northern Panama, she could make it as well as many other meals. There, a young girl could cook very well by the age of seven or eight. Jim threw his coat on the custom-made Italian white leather couch. He greeted Rosa with the familiar kiss and a "what's for eat?"

"I made you some arroz con pollo, veijo," she called him this, not in the derogatory sense but lovingly and affectionately.

"What happened to your hand?" she asked, concerned.

"Smacked it one some cowling," he replied, thinking nothing of it. Rosa was stirring a pot on the stove.

"Why don't you put something on that?" she said.

Jim looked at her and raised an eyebrow. A smile came across his face. He didn't say a word, he knew better. Going upstairs immediately, he returned in a couple of minutes with "something on it."

Dinner was on the table. Rosa called the kids, and they all sat down and ate. As Jim worked on putting away the dishes, he told Rosa about his day.

"After work today, Bud and I went over the Clinton for a couple of beers. Got to go down to the yacht club for a few hours tonight also. Something's cooking, and I'll tell you about it when I get back."

Rosa looked at him suspiciously. The last time he did that, Bud decided to take the boat out, and it wasn't going anywhere Jim had already decided to limit it to the club and then back home. By now, it was eight o'clock, so Jim took off for downtown DC.

CHAPTER 4

Capital Yacht Club

Pulling out of the apartment complex, Jim turned on the radio and headed for the district. At this time of night, there wasn't very much traffic into Washington. Everyone was leaving and going home or was already there. As he drove down the parkway, he thought to himself how pretty it was. It was nothing like what was over the bridge. Over there were what looked like crack houses on every block. In vacant bottom floor apartment buildings, people hung out nightly.

"Don't want to break down here," he thought aloud.

Changing the radio stations, looking for some rock and roll, he caught the end of an old song. Some guy sang about being stuck down in Honduras and needing lawyers, guns, and money "cause the shit has hit the fan."

"Catchy tune," he said to himself, "have to remember that one."

Before long, he was at the parking area across from the yacht club. He turned down the ramp and pulled up next to Bud's car in the underground reserved parking area. As he looked up, Charlie, the night security guard, walked by.

"Bud's up dockside on his cell phone that came with a large battery pack in a briefcase-size bag."

"All right, thanks!" Jim returned. "Hey, keep an eye on my car, okay?"

Charlie waved, and Jim went up the stairs. At the top, Jim spotted Bud by the pier gate. Out at the end of the pier was where the yacht was kept. Bud's was on the very end across from some rather impressive-looking toys of the rich and famous. Bud's yacht wasn't shabby either. At around sixty feet, it was quite comfortable. As Jim walked up, Bud was just finishing up his conversation.

"Okay, then it's set, Saturday and Sunday. No more than six people. Yes, two security also. Well, see you then, take care." Bud looked at Jim. "Hey, man, let's get a drink. Talking to these guys makes me thirsty."

Sometimes Bud lent out his services to local hotshot lobbyists that sometimes liked to entertain discreetly. This was one those deals. Upon reaching a table close to the main bar, they sat, and within minutes Colonel Moran showed up. He was dressed in civilian clothes, and neither Bud or Jim noticed him approach until he was right there. After exchanging the usual common courtesies, they all sat down. Colonel Moran looked down at his watch, a gold Rolex.

"I don't have too much time to spend here, so I'll get right to the point. There's a civilian aircraft operation down in Panama working out of Howard Air Force Base. They have a contract with the Department of Defense to provide logistics support to SOUTHCOM. They operate out of there and up-country at Soto Cano Air Base, Comayagua, Honduras.

"The name of the company is Evergreen Helicopters. Its parent company is Evergreen International, with corporate offices in McMinnville, Oregon. They also maintain a site at Marana, Arizona. Basically they are doing the same mission that Southern Air Transport has done in the past, except on a smaller, more inconspicuous way. If you call this number, they might offer you a trip over to talk about working for them."

Jim took the piece of paper and put it in his pocket.

"I've got a question before I go dropping a quarter in the box," Jim asked. "What's the situation down there right now?"

Colonel Moral answered, "Same as always. Nothing you can't handle. Besides, you've got as much on what's going on as I do. It's just like any other time or place you've been."

What the colonel meant was, it was a "civilian" operation, with none of the agency people involved directly. Of course, if they needed something, they would know who to contact and how to go about it.

Bud just smiled as he rested his chin in his hands with his elbows on the table. Colonel Moran started to leave.

"Uh, Dick! What's the benefit package on this?" Jim asked.

The colonel answered him as he scooted his chair back under the table. "Benefit package! Hasn't changed as far as I know—same deal, same pay."

Jim, with a queer look on his face, remembered all too well the other times. Benefit zero, zip, nada. That is unless they needed something, and then it would be on a case-by-case need. Of course, if Jim needed a favor or needed to expedite something, this could be accomplished rather easily with just a phone call.

"Well, you got the ball," Colonel Moran said with a unique smile on his face. He knew what Jim wanted, and he knew Jim had been after a Panama assignment for years. "Oh, I'll give you this right off. When and if you make the jump down south, don't get too far out like you did in Turkey. Something's going down and real soon. I can't let you in on what, but if you don't want to be tied down and put on the spot or involved in something that you won't have much control over, don't hang out south of the bridge." Col Moran turned and left.

Jim and Bud sat there quietly until he was gone.

"South of the bridge! Damn! Just when you thought it was safe to go back to the beach," Jim said.

Bud interrupted, "What's south of the bridge?"

Jim started in on a geography lesson. He told Bud that Panama City was south of the bridge. The bridge is called Thatcher Ferry Bridge, named after the ferry whose place it took. Spanning the Panama Canal on the Pacific side, it is also called Puente De Las Americas. Built back in the sixties, the bridge made crossing the canal easy. Now there were no long waiting lines waiting for the ferry. He then went on to explain that Panama City wasn't really on the south side as most people thought. The Republic of Panama is an isthmus, and it has a short of *S* shape to it. The Canal Zone and the Panama Canal itself actually run sort of north and south.

After Jim told Bud that, he started looking funny. Then to make matters even more confusing, he told Bud that Panama City was on the east side and ran around a semicircle coast on the Pacific. Jim could remember many times back in the seventies when he would be over at Farfan Beach or Venado Beach when the sun came up in the morning.

"Yes, the sun comes up on the Pacific Ocean," he told Bud, who by this time was perplexed by the whole conversation.

Downtown Washington, as Jim called it, was quite a place. You never know who or what you would run into. This place was no different. Bud was a veteran yacht club member and got to meet all sorts of varied people in all sorts of varied states of intoxication.

"Hey, you know what I heard in here the other day?" Bud blurts out.

"No telling, but I'm sure I'm about to find out," Jim responds. Bud started to relate a conversation he just happened to overhear. Seems these two or three well-dressed guys sporting fifteen-hundred-dollar suits and ten-thousand-dollar Rolexes had had a little too much liquor and were just a little too loud. Bud, being just a little to close, had gotten an earful. These individuals, as Bud told it, were discussing the feasibility and/or need of the federal government creating a national police force, NPF for short. According to what was overheard, they would operate similar to federal marshals except that there would be more.

As Bud put it, "Man, what a spooky thought, secret police."

Bud went on and on, but Jim was thinking about the piece of paper that Colonel Moran had given him. He told Bud that tomorrow was a workday so he had better take off and head to the hooch. Bud went out to the yacht and Jim to his car. Jim figured to sleep on what was said and decided what to do in the morning. Having been in or through over sixty countries over the past twenty years, he didn't need much sleep to decide. He liked to travel. It probably started when he was a child. His parents would take summer vacations to the west and up into Canada. He visited his uncle Gene once in Churchill, Manitoba, Canada. Uncle Gene lived right up on the Hudson Bay. As Jim got older, he liked the excitement, adventure, the thrill of the unknown. Jim had been to places retirees save a lifetime for just to go for a week. He didn't play the tourist role, though.

He liked to get down with the locals—eat what they eat, wear what they wear, talk like they talk, live like they live. He had been places no other American had been. He had been places no other American had ever wanted to go. This was what he thrived on. The honor to say, "Been there, done that!"

He could recall events and describe areas from back alleys of Bangkok to the loud, smelly twenty-four-hour market in Cairo. He had scuba dived in Malta and skydived in Chad. As Jim would say, "I've been shot at and missed, shit at and hit, been around the world ten times, two country fairs, and a donkey show. What's the holdup? Let's do it. Just another day in paradise!"

By now he was almost home and just that much closer to a nice comfortable warm bed. The temperature was dropping again, but the weather man wasn't calling for snow. If it snowed, chances were he couldn't have to go to work tomorrow.

Jim didn't really care anyway. His job out at Andrews was a piece of cake. The aircraft, Beechcraft King Airs, were well maintained by a group of every experienced field reps. They seldom broke. The shop was run by a retired chief master sergeant named Joe Chappel. He had retired with thirty-plus years. Beech Aerospace Services Inc. had hired him to act as site supervisor at the naval air facility at Andrews. Chappel had been the chief flight engineer on *Air Force One*. He had been on the plane when Kennedy was shot in Dallas. He had friends everywhere. Sometime he would get a call and go play golf with Ford. Although he knew Pentagon generals by first name, he was a legend in his eyes only.

BASI kept him around for political reasons. Jim thought of him like an old encyclopedia, very valuable when you needed some info, but most of the time just dead weight, collecting dust on the shelf. All the work on the planes was done by the other guys: Ron Weight, John Merle, Glenn Kahler, and Jim.

Just like Senior Chief Schelinberger (Shelly), who was the chief flight engineer for Admiral Gallo, who was Chief of Naval Operations Mediterranean, they both were good in their day but had been replaced by the new "young guns" who were more qualified and could handle the ever faster jets.

As the smoke-belching old radial engine powered aircraft were retired and sent to the bone yard, so were their crews, replaced by technology and progress.

Jim had just passed the front gate to Andrews AFB. He turned in the apartment complex and parked his car.

CHAPTER 5

Andrews Air Force Base

Waiting in line and inching forward at a turtle's pace toward the front gate of Andrews Air Force base, Jim rubbed his eyes. The night before had been one of those sleepless nights that on occasion attacks everyone. The gate guard waved him through. Jim drove slowly around to the navy side of Andrews. He worked in the first hangar of the Beech Aerospace Services Inc., a defense contractor on the navy C-12 Program. Basically it was a contract that provided logistical support to the various aircraft assigned to the Commander Marine Corps Aviation.

Beech Aerospace was this contractor who provided this service. The on-site liaison officer was the base commander; however, the controlling authority was Naval Air Logistics Command, Pentagon, Washington, DC. Jim had been working this assignment for only a little less than a year now. He had been reassigned to Washington after completing a three-year contract at the naval air facility in Sigonella, Sicily. Just a short distance outside Catania on the island of Sicily, the air facility was on the north side of an Italian NATO base. Over there, he worked on the same type of program but was under the command of Admiral Gallo, Chief of Naval Operations Med. Unlike Naples to the north, Sigonella was a hot spot of a place to work. Here was a military base just a few hundred miles north of Africa and situated at the base of Mount Etna. The never-ending column of smoke puffing out like a locomotive and never let you forget that she was there. It was an ominous sight. At over ten thousand feet, it took up most of the northern horizon. Sometimes it belched out more than smoke, as the Sicilians all too well knew. Many times Jim had come to work and brushed off cinders as large as marbles from the top of the aircraft wings. Sometimes he just stopped and pondered the force it must have took to sling these cinders some forty miles down to the base. Sometimes he didn't have time to ponder anything but what was happening at the moment. Being assigned to Sigonella from 1985 to 1988, he was there when Colonel Gaddafi was stirring up problems in the area. There had been the incident with the Achille Lauro and then there was the terrorist hijacking in March 1985. If it wasn't a bomb threat, which occurred all the frequently, it was the terrorist stirring up some shit. If that wasn't enough, every now and then, the damn mountain blew up, spitting rock, cinders, and red-hot lava down the side toward the towns below. Today Belpasso, tomorrow Zaffarini, next time maybe Paternò. Jim remembered one night watching the forever occurring fireworks display the Sicilians loved to shoot off on any and every occasion. Once a crack shot up the wall, and the front room chandelier started jumping around. The windows in the French doors to the balcony rattled and cracked. Jim was awestruck. That night there was the volcano erupting in the distance, street level fireworks display, and topped off with a real live earthquake. Only war could match the action. Jim compared Sicily to Texas, both situated kind of down at the bottom of the country and on the water. Sicilians still rode around on scooters with shotguns strapped over their shoulders, kind of like a Texan in a truck with a gun rack. Sicily has a personality about it. Sicily was unique and very different from mainland Italy to the north. Jim liked it there and took to it like a duck takes to water.

He remembered the Libyan crisis back in 1988. The confrontation and the ending, so to speak, with the F-111 bombing of downtown Tripoli: The air force had been flying the F-111's to Sigonella on a regular basis for maybe a month prior to the bombing. Then one day on the way in, they didn't stop. They just kept on going and after getting rid of some added weight, came back and stopped in for a while.

Jim, still rubbing his eyes, pulled into the parking lot. He jumped out and headed for Hangar One to go to work, thinking to himself, *Man what a night! Things going a little fast or what! Fast! You ain't seen fast! Just wait till I get rolling, then you'll see fast. Nothing but elbows and assholes. Speaking of assholes.* Jim cuts himself off as he enters the office. *Blam!* The door slams loudly as it closes with help from the wind. Joe was sitting there behind his old funky desk with a look of complacency on his face.

"Hey, Joe, what's shakin'?" Jim greeted him.

Joe, off in never-never land, looks up. "Nothing much, just a couple of wash jobs. The other guys are already out on the hangar deck."

Jim glanced at the clock on the wall. It was 0630. "Man, half an hour early and the other guys were already at it. I thought I was fast!" Jim remarked under his breath.

He walked out on the hangar deck. Jim eyed the familiar sleek, spotless C-12 King Airs. *Beechcraft sure makes a fine airplane*, he thought to himself.

About that time, John Merle came around the back of aircraft 206.

"Hey, Jim, called your house this morning to see if you wanted to start early. Start early, get out early. Wife said you had already left for work."

He was dragging a water hose around to start the next wing. "Yeah, right," Jim replied.

What a bunch of shit. That morning, as every morning, Jim had dropped his wife off at work on the way into work. "Hey, Merle, what's that brown stuff on your nose? I know it can't be a grease, 'cause I ain't never seen you in these wheel wells!" Jim said.

John just smiles and wiped his nose with his fist. Later Jim was soaping down one of the wheel wells and mumbling to himself, "What a bunch of butt holes. Joe starts at 0630, so why come in at 0530? It's just a couple of wash jobs, not like we have an o'dark thirty launch with Poindexter and North on board. Got to get those brownie points, I guess. After all, they are the ones that will be here forever, not me."

Jim finished up cleaning the wheel well area and slid over to the other side. It was easy work, sitting on a roll-around chair. It was dirty work, though. Jim didn't care. If he got real dirty and greasy, then he wouldn't have to go anywhere the big shots were.

"Have to keep up the professional image you know," Joe would say.

As Jim finished up the last wheel well area, John and Ron Weight rolled up the hoses and dumped the wash buckets. Joe finally came out of the office, and everyone wiped down the planes. They looked good. It was almost lunchtime, so everybody retired to the break room to eat. After everyone got started, Joe asked who wanted to stay late and wax the planes. Jim offered to stay. He knew that if he did, he would probably get cut back early tomorrow or, better yet, not even have to come in.

Then he would hang out over at Potomac Field with Bud. He had a hundred-hour inspection to do on a Queen Air, so he wouldn't be off for nothing. The two jobs worked well together. The Andrews job was salary, and the Potomac job was contract. It made for some liberties he wouldn't have if he had to punch a clock. Just about through with lunch, Joe said, "Okay, Jim, wax them down and go home. Merle will help you. Take tomorrow off. If I need you, I'll call or beep you."

With that, Joe and Ron Weight took off. Andrews was a lot different than the overseas sites. Here they received a flight schedule a week in advance. You could plan things that way. At Sigonella, you were lucky if you even got a schedule. Those times when you did, it turned out to be no good, usually. Always a change at the last minute. Jim didn't know if it was because of the ever-present terrorist threat or just plain old operations incompetence. John and Jim went back out on the hangar deck, grabbing the wax bottles as they went. Merle asked Jim what the news was around town. He knew Jim had a line to the inside. John's wife was a GS-12 or something and worked in the district. Exactly where, John would never say, but he would come up with some of the wildest things. It was like if John already knew the answer, and if someone else knew also, then his info was confirmed. Jim answered the question with a simple, "Beats me, you're the one with all the answers, Oh Great and Powerful Oz!"

John made a funny face. It didn't take long to do the planes. After all, they were not that big, and they were pretty good at this waxing thing, having done it for years.

"Well, that about does it," Jim remarked, standing back at the rear of the hangar.

"Let's get out of here before something happens," John answers.

They put their tools up dumped the trash, gave the floor the once-over with the mop, and left. Jim drove over to the other side of the base. He parked in the NCO Club parking lot and went in to see what was on MTV. He liked to watch MTV and have a couple of beers to relax before going home. After sitting for a while, he took out a piece of paper and pen. He was always jotting down something important that he might want to remember later. Jim was happy, or at least he was contented.

The Crash

Jim was still in bed when the phone rang. He had been awake but was just lying there thinking. Rosa was downstairs in the kitchen. After about four rings, he hollered down, "Somebody get that phone already! You know it might be important." There was no answer. "Oh well, if it's Joe, the beeper will go off in a minute."

Just then the answering machine cut on. He had forgotten that it was on. "Hello, can't come to the phone right now, busy. Leave your name and number, and I'll call you back as soon as I can." *Beeep!*

Jim, still in bed, was making pictures out of the rough textured ceiling paint. *Let's see, that one looks like a dog, and that one looks like an old man with glasses*, Jim thought. Straining to hear the message being left, he just sat there. He couldn't quite make it out, but it definitely wasn't Joe. It was a woman's voice. He was now getting up.

She said, "This is Linda, personnel manager for Evergreen Helicopters, McMinnville Oregon. Sorry it took so long to get back to you. It's been real busy here lately. Anyway, we would like to talk to you about the CASA Program. I'll be in my office all day. So if you could, give me a call. I've got a few questions to ask you. Thanks."

Jim had come downstairs and played the message just yesterday. Rosa was still in the kitchen. He went inside to see what was in the fridge. Standing there with a gallon of milk in his hand, he wondered where he had put the current updated resume he had made up last week. Jim was looking around the house.

"Sweetheart, have you seen my briefcase?"

Rosa told him it was under the stairs with some other junk that didn't have a place.

Jim dug around and came up with it.

"Want to eat?" Rosa asked.

"Yeah, I'm starved." Jim woke up hungry. He always woke up hungry. Breakfast was perfect—scrambled eggs, bacon and patacones. Patacones were something he had acquired a taste for many years ago during that first trip down south. They were made out of plantain bananas, green ones. Most Panamanians ate patacones every day for breakfast.

"Hey, look, I'm going out to Potomac this morning, so if Bud calls, I've already left, okay?"

Rosa asked if he needed a lunch. He didn't. Usually on Saturdays, they ate at the field, sometimes barbeque or maybe go into Clinton for some clam chowder.

Jim finished up breakfast, showered, and came back downstairs. Rosa had packed a lunch anyway. She always did. He knew she would. Rosa loved him and was always concerned about him not getting enough to eat. By now the kids were in front of the TV for Saturday morning cartoons, standard procedure for kids on Saturday mornings.

Once out at Potomac, he would update his resume and fax it out to McMinnville. During the drive out, he daydreamed about the upcoming weeks ahead. He wondered what the pay package would be. He wondered what kind of expense account he would have. The mission. Size of operation. Scope of contract. Was it going to be accompanied status or not? Hazardous duty pay? There were a lot of questions he needed to know the answers to before he made any commitment. He especially needed to know about the pay. It's good to know what you were going to be paid before you get off the plane and step into a full-blown raging battle, only to later find out the pay sucked. He stopped at the 7-Eleven to buy some gas and a can of Copenhagen. Then down the hill to the airstrip. As he drove through the residential area, he wondered what would happened today.

Just then, he crested the top of the hill and saw Bud's car and a few more down below. They were parked in front of the hangar, and Bud was talking to a couple of guys. Jim recognized one of them as Larry Hahn. Bud had introduced Jim to Larry a month or so previous. That was back when they were setting up the operation at Potomac. Larry worked for Aero Service Aviation down in Miami, Florida. Larry also worked out at Andrews AFB. He flew one of the unmarked 707s that were parked close to where Jim worked. Larry would come up to DC for a while and then back to Florida. Jim never knew when he would show up or for how long. Larry stayed pretty tight-lipped, considering what he did and who he worked for. Jim parked beside the hangar and walked over to where everybody was standing.

"Hey, Jimbo! Larry exclaimed. He stuck out his hand.

"How long you up for this time?" Jim asked him.

"Oh, I don't know. Week, maybe two," Larry replied.

"Great! Maybe later on we can get together and shoot the shit."

Bud jumped in, "Shoot some beers, don't you know."

Jim glanced over at the other guy there. He didn't recognize him, but if he was hanging with Bud and Larry, he was surely okay.

Bud caught Jim's look and introduced the stranger.

"Jim, this is a good friend of mine. Say hello to Skip Palmengren." Skip was a local deputy sheriff for Prince George County. Since it was Saturday and he was off, he had stopped by to see about renting out one of Bud's aircraft. It seemed he wanted to go up and fly over a suspected pot field about fifteen miles south of Potomac. He knew about it and where it was supposed to be from a tip. He figures it was worth checking out and Bud's J-3 Cub wouldn't draw any attention.

"Little nippy out here today. How about we go inside and get some coffee," Larry suggested.

They all went back to the office at the back of the hangar. As Bud and Skip talked, Jim and Larry made coffee.

"Bud tells me we've got a guy bringing over a Queen Air from Easton today," Larry says.

"Oh yeah, what time?"

"He said this morning. I'd expect around ten or so. He needs an annual inspections and just might hangar it here—that is, if we treat him right," Larry said loud enough so Bud could hear.

Larry was also a Federal Aviation Administration Inspector and signed off the logs after Jim and his crew fixed the write-ups and performed the required maintenance.

"Skip, how you like your mud?" Larry hollers over.

"Bud says he likes his like his women, strong and black."

Bud just sat there. He wasn't amused. After a couple of cups, Skip had to go. He would be back in the early afternoon, though. As Bud and Larry talked, Skip and Jim walked back up to the front to where the cars parked.

"Bud tells me you're the chief of maintenance out here, and if you want anything done, just get with you and you'll take care of it," Skip asked.

"Well, I'll try, but it depends on what it is and what it is will determine how long it takes," he replied.

Just then, Larry and Bud came out the hangar door. Spotting a flash of light in the east, Bud squinted. "Maybe that's our Queen Air coming in," he said as he pointed toward a black dot on the horizon.

"If it is, he's way wide on the approach," Larry remarked as if he had been in that same situation at least once before. The black dot, now a lot closer, was really wide. They began to think that it wasn't even coming there but going over the Clinton Airfield. Just before it went out of the sight behind the tree line at the end of the runway, it veered back hard and was now way wide in the opposite direction. All four of them were watching with great concern as the aircraft again overcorrects and banks hard to line up on the runway.

"Man, he's high and hot! Better do a go-around and line back up for a better shot or he won't make it," Larry said from years of experience. He had concern written all over his face. The Queen Air came up and over the runway and by midfield wasn't on the deck, or even close. By that time the pilot realized that he wouldn't be able to get her down and stopped. He poured the coals to her. Just as the engines started to wind up, there was a loud *whoop*, then silence. The most feared event the pilot could experience just happened. He was about a hundred feet above the ground, out of runway, trees dead ahead and no power! The plane passed over and dropped out of sight behind a vacant trailer that was alongside the hangar.

They stood there with disbelief on their faces, with mouths wide open and not being able to move. There came a low, loud muffled *booom!*

"Shit! Goddamnit! Shit! Shit! Shit! The son of a bitch crashed," Jim was shouting. In an instant he was running toward the airplane. All kinds of thoughts were racing through his mind as he ran as fast as he could. What would he find? Fire? Dead People? Body parts? All he could do was get there and get the pilot out and whoever else might be there, out. Bud had run inside the hangar to call 911 and the fire department.

At about a hundred yards from the crumpled mass of plane, Skip and Larry caught up with Jim in Skip's car. When Jim took off running, they had jumped into their car and sped down the runway. They were now honking and waving for Jim to get in. A few seconds passed, and they screeched to a stop just in front of the downed aircraft. It had bellied in and skidded to a stop in heavy brush. It wasn't on fire. Jim ran up to the cabin door and yelled inside. There was smoke everywhere, and he coughed.

"You okay?" Jim yelled again. He waved his arms to clear smoke.

The pilot yelled back, "Yeah!"

"Well then, get the fuck outta here before it catches fire, you dumb shit!" He had blood on his head. Jim and Skip helped him over the seats. There was trash everywhere, and it smelled of fuel and burning wire. The pilot, at least was walking, no broken bones. None that he could see anyway. He might have been a "dumb shit," but he was a lucky dumb shit. After all, he was walking, and any time you land and walk away, it was good landing. Maybe not for the aircraft, but for you it was good. Jim made his way to the cockpit amid a pile of debris an all sorts of stuffs that breaks loosed when you "pop the ground." He turned off the fuel boost pumps and electrical master switch. Since it wasn't smoking or sizzling, it probably wouldn't catch fire, at least he hoped not. At least not until the fire crew got there, so if it did, they could put it out.

After securing the switches, Jim climbed back out over the buckled seats. There were cushions and clothes in the aisle. Jim proceeded toward the rear air stair door where someone one was yelling to get out now!

Too bad there was a cop present for all this, Jim thought momentarily. *Could have laid down under a wing and started moaning about this plane falling out of the sky on me. For sure screwing up my back. That ought to be good for a couple of bucks.* Naw, he had other plans in the works, and it probably wouldn't work anyway. Just as Jim got around to the nose radome area, the boys in yellow showed up.

"Everybody back! Get back! Get back before it blows!" yelled the guys in charge.

"Only thing that will blow around here is the wind up the street," Jim mumbles, barely audible but enough that the head honcho heard him.

"Who the hell are you?" the fire captain snapped. Skip jumped in and defused the possible situation. He told the big banana that Jim was a Beechcraft field rep and the best authority on this type of aircraft for a hundred miles. Since Skip was an officer, the fire captain changed his tone. As the EMS crew sped off to the hospital with "Crash," a name that would later stick, Skip and Jim gave the firemen a brief on what had happened. After they roped off the impact area and the plane with yellow "Do Not Cross" tape, everyone went back to the hangar. Sitting in Skip's car, still a little shaken from what had just transpired, Jim remarked, "You know this inspection is gonna cost this guy a pretty penny!"

By now it was past lunchtime, so Skip took off, and the rest of the guys headed out to Clinton Inn for burgers. *Never a dull day*, Jim thought. He wondered what the afternoon would bring. Maybe "buzz" a pot field and have a gun battle with a bunch of dope-dealing smugglers. Then again maybe not. He had all the fun he could stand for one day. Tomorrow was a different story, though.

Loose Ends

The sun beat down from a cloudless sky, making the phone booth ever increasingly warmer till it was almost downright hot. Jim had to make a phone call and didn't want anyone at BASI to overhear the conversation. After being put on hold for what seemed a good long while, Linda answered.

"Jim, glad to hear from you. I got your resume that you faxed me last Sunday. I've just got a few questions to ask you and then we can make arrangements for you to come in and talk to us and do paperwork."

"Sure, what do you want to know?" Jim responded.

"Well, I see you've worked overseas programs before. Some pretty interesting ones too, I might add," she said.

Jim thought to himself, *No kidding, does a bear crap in the woods or what?*

"What I need to know is, how does your family feel about going overseas?" she asked.

Jim told her it wouldn't be a problem. "Matter of fact, my wife is overseas right now!" he told her.

Linda was puzzled. To elaborate, he told her that his wife was Panamanian and was here in the States, so she was technically overseas by being out of her country. He assured Linda that, in her case, it would be more like going home.

"Oh, okay! I can see that. When can you come up?" she asked. Jim told her he could be in her office Monday morning. He had the weekend duty and would have Monday and Tuesday off. He planned on flying out on Sunday night and do what needed to be done on Monday. Then he would fly back to DC on Tuesday. Linda said that it sounded good and she would make arrangements that week. With the details all worked out, he told her that he would see her on Monday. Since it was lunch break, Joe, John, Ron, and Glenn were all in the office eating when Jim came back in.

"What up, Jim? Did you call your girlfriend and didn't want us to listen in?" Joe queried. These guys didn't have a clue.

"Nope, had to call my broker and see what the price of import coffee is doing." Jim smiled as he answered back quickly.

"Why? You planning on buying out Juan Valdez or something?" John Merle said smartly. Ron and Glen just kept on eating. They usually didn't have much to say about anything. Glen Kaler was always quiet. Unless you asked him a question, he never added much to the conversation. He sometimes raised an eyebrow a little. Joe told everyone that Ed Schnieder was on the phone earlier and was planning on coming up to present us with a plaque and commendation for our outstanding performance. Ed Schnieder was the vice-president of Beech Aerospace Services Inc. located down in Madison, Mississippi. The navy was having a change of command ceremony, and evidently the commander going out wanted to show his appreciation by letting the main office present us with commendations endorsed by him.

Oh, this is just great, Jim thought. *One day get an "attaboy" and the next day quit!* Well, at least Jim was going out on good terms. Ever since that dipshit Steve Guidorsy came to Sigonella, Sicily, where Jim was assigned prior to Washington, DC, Jim had been on one of the program administrator's shit list. Of course, it would take more than one attaboy to overcome all the smoke that Steve had blown up Ralph Kinnard's ass. From the very first day when Steve had arrived in Italy, he proved he couldn't handle it. He screwed things up so bad that nothing short of a complete personnel change would fix it. He was transferred, and Jim had taken the heat. This got Jim to Washington. It had been a year since Jim had been reassigned from the Mediterranean, and he was still pissed off. He had lost a lot of money in the move and now wasn't even where the action was. He sensed he was just treading water and just waiting for something to break loose or start up. Little did he know, it had already started. As they say, the proverbial shit was fixin' to hit the fan.

After work, Jim went straight home. He wanted to see how far Rosa and the kids had gotten on the packing. He had made arrangements for Patuxent River Storage to come and pick up the furniture and items not going down. They would be there on Wednesday of next week. Every time Jim moved, it was the same thing—put most of it in storage and the rest, box it and mail it through the US Postal Services base to base insured.

Giving a thirty-day lead time, he was usually set up in country before the boxes started to arrive. He mailed them, all thirty or so, to Howard Air Force Base, Panama. Insuring each for about five hundred dollars, Jim dared the post office to loose just one. The rest of the week went by as usual. Nothing out of the ordinary happened. He just tied up loose ends and made plans on what he was going to do on Monday.

That cold, damp, foggy Monday morning, Jim arrived by cab at the Evergreen Helicopters office in McMinnville, Oregon. As he walked through the front door and approached the receptionist, he remarked to himself how nice the place looked. It looked more like a lawyer's office or maybe the grand lobby of a large hotel. One thing for sure, it didn't look like any aircraft operation that Jim had been associated with before.

After a cup of coffee and short wait, Linda arrived and introduced herself. They went to her office, and after completing the required paperwork, she took him around the place. She showed him the operation, and Jim was impressed. He learned that Evergreen had all kinds of sticks in the fire. The owner of Evergreen was a self-made millionaire, and it showed. They had a UPS contract to deliver parcels, a fire-fighting operation up in the mountains and in Alaska. There was also a Black Fly Eradication Program contracted to the World Health Organization based over in the "toolies" Africa. The company was also involved with some government contracts down in Central and South America. Jim assumed it was support for the DEA.

They had some pretty good programs going on, he thought to himself. Although Evergreen was doing work in most, if not all, Central American countries, the CASA Program was what Jim was most interested in. The CASA Program was based out of Howard Air Force Base, Panama. It also had a sister site up in Comayagua, Honduras at Soto Cano Air Base. The base used to be called Palmerola Air Base but had recently been changed to Soto Cano Air Base, named after a General Soto Cano of the Honduran Army. Evergreen kept three aircraft at Howard Air Force Base and two others at Comayagua. Every two weeks or so, they would rotate aircrews and aircraft up to Honduras in support of army operations there and up-country. The casas were medium-size aircraft. They were built in Madrid, Spain. Since the aircraft were European, they were metric. Jim overlooked this aspect of contract. With all the logistics of the move going on, he didn't realize that they would require special metric tools. Jim had thousands of dollars' worth of tools, but they were all American standard, mostly Snap-on tools. The Casa 212s were a high-wing STOL (short field takeoff and landing) capable airplane with fixed down landing gear. Equipped with Garret 331 turbo prop engines and rear ramp similar to those on a C-130s with two engines. The inside could be configured to a cargo bay or to troop transport with web seats. Capable of short field takeoffs and landings, they were perfect for what they were assigned to do. The contract was for logistics support, and that meant, "Whatever, whoever, wherever."

"Man, this looks interesting," Jim said.

"A Spanish-built aircraft that can operate out of the shortest of fields, no N number (US registration number), no American flag on the tail, strange indeed. This and a civilian-run operation providing logistics for the army as well as other government entitles in Central America. Based on an air force base with up-country off-site operations in Honduras."

"Yeah, this sounds like the man," Jim said as he smiled.

Linda told him that they were assembling a group, even as they spoke. Everyone would meet up in Anchorage, Alaska, for a familiarization course on the aircraft and briefing on the aircraft operations, then fly down to Panama. The advance party was already there. They had the operation set up and fully on line. The second group would be them. Things were finally beginning to pick up. Jim was excited, to say the least. He had been trying to get back to Panama for years, and now it was coming together real good, or so he thought.

That afternoon, he caught the late flight back to DC. When he got home, he had a long talk with his wife, Rosa. She wasn't all that thrilled with the trip. She had just been down there last summer, and Noriega was really stirring up the shit with the Americans, as well as the local Panamanians. The country was under martial law, and the military ruled by sheer force, intimidation, and repression. Last summer, while Rose was visiting her aunt in San Andreas, Chriqui, the local "La Guardia" brought her in for questioning. After a couple of hours or so, they were satisfied and let her leave, but she didn't like it one bit. Jim reassured her that there wouldn't be a problem this time. If it did turn bad, they could always just leave. Jim was counting on his contacts to give him some heads-up notice of impending danger. She finally agreed, and that was that. Jim knew she would.

"So now what?" Rosa asked.

"Well, tomorrow I let BASI know my intentions and then Saturday, it's off to Alaska. Be back the next Saturday, and then first thing Monday morning, we head south," advised Jim.

The rest of the week, Jim and Rosa boxed and mailed their gear and whatever items they would need to set up a household in Panama. He told BASI of his intentions, and surprisingly enough it didn't cause too much of a ruckus. Ralph Kinnard had changed jobs with Bob Stinson, one of the other program administrators.

It didn't matter to Jim. They all lied as well as the other. Bob had one of his "brown noses" call Jim to confirm the termination date. In all, it went pretty smoothly. Now everything was set. He had cleaned out all his equipment at Potomac Air Field and shipped it to McMinnville. He had said his goodbyes to the guys. Next week, the packers would come while he was up in Anchorage. When he got back, he would pick up the suitcases, Rosa, the kids and proceed to Panama. Jim was a master at this kind of relocation. He had gotten it down to a fine art; everything looked good to go as planned.

The Great Seat Affair

Jim had gotten up early and was getting ready to finished up the last part of packing for Anchorage. Standing in the kitchen, he was drinking a cup of coffee and talking to Rosa. The phone rang, and it was Bud. Rosa was cooking breakfast, and as Jim spoke on the phone, she strained to hear what was being said. Jim hung up, and turning to Rosa, he said he had to go out to Potomac. Something had come up, and Bud needed him for a short while. Jim drove right out to see what the big emergency was.

After he got out there and talked to Bud, he found out what the deal was. It seemed that the previous morning, as prearranged, Skip had arrived out at Potomac. He and Bud had decided to do the pot field flyby, or flyover, as the case would be.

Bud not only had a J-3 Piper Cub, he owned several other aircraft as well. Instead of going out in the J-3, they decided to go up in the Stearman biplane. The Stearman was an open cockpit, bi-wing fabric aircraft of the World War I vintage. It had the power to get up fast, plus it was fully aerobatic.

Jim had been up a couple of times with Bud. It was great. The big blue-and-yellow navy trainer was sweet, even if it did look like a crop duster. Bud liked to consider himself quite the "barnstormer." He dressed the part, complete with leathers and goggles. Well, Skip was excited, to say the least. Here he thought he was going up in a fully enclosed, warm, really slow airplane. Now he was going to play "Snoopy vs. Red Baron."

Bud assumed Skip knew the aircraft capabilities. Mainly, it could fly upside down as well as it could right side up.

They got suited up. With overalls on, they climbed up on the wing. Skip got up front. This was the usual place for a student or passenger—that is, unless you thought they might get sick. If so, you would put them in the rear cockpit. That way, you wouldn't get anything on you. Bud was a pretty good judge of who would and who wouldn't; he told of more than one occasion of where his rider barfed and really ruined the day. Skip had told Bud that he had a cast-iron stomach and had never thrown up. Bud let him stay up front.

After they got airborne, it was only a couple of minutes over to the inspection area. Skip gave directions, and Bud flew about eight hundred feet above the highway. It was easier to just follow the road. You never get lost that way, Bud used to say. He had his own way of doing things. He used to say they put the town name on water towers so you would know where you were. Chicken houses always were built east and west. They were build that way so the morning and afternoon sun wouldn't shine in. Chickens will die if they got too hot. On cold windy days, cows would always face into the wind. These are the things that the old-time pilots knew to get around the countryside without getting lost. Jim remembered one day Bud had asked him how he would fly in the fog. How would you get down and land? Jim didn't have any idea. Bud told him that you take a cat and duck up with you. If you got disoriented, you take the out the cat and throw it up a couple of times. Since a cat always lands on its feet, that was down. Then throw out the duck and follow it down. When it starts to flare out to land, get ready, you were too. You might have a fifty-fifty chance it would be on water, but don't worry, ducks never land in trees. Bud was laughing by then. Sometimes Jim wondered about him.

Bud and Skip made it over to the area of suspicion and started doing some low-level passes. After a while, and no pot field, they gave up and headed back to the field. Skip was pretty bummed out about the whole situation. Bud thought he would cheer him up with some maneuvers and aerobatics. Bud hollered up and to Skip, and when he turned around, Bud showed him some hand signals meaning he was getting ready to do tricks. He must have looked weird to Skip, who just gave him the thumbs up. He thought Bud wanted to know how he was doing. At that, Bud pulls the stick back and applies the power. Straight up they go, about three hundred feet. Bud leveled off, and Skip is all smiles. Bud said later that he looked like an opossum-eating prickly pear. After a few minutes of straight and level flight, Skip turned around and gave Bud the thumbs-up sign.

"He was really enjoying this," Bud related.

Since there wasn't a problem, Bud decided to put it inverted for a little upside-down attitude. He snap rolled it over to the right and stopped perfectly, upside down. Everything was going along fine until Bud's seat decided to let go. The latch opened, and gravity took effect. It wasn't because of shoddy maintenance or defective equipment. The seat was just well used, worn from many, many years of service.

Bud said, "All of a sudden, the son of a bitch let go. Clickity, clickity, clickity, pow."

The last *pow* was the seat hitting the full high seat stops.

The Stearman was used for navy military flight training. The seat was able to be adjusted for any height pilot. It could accommodate the tallest to the very shortest. Bud was in the latter group. When the seat let loose and went to the fully extended position, it left Bud about halfway out of the cockpit.

"Nearly gave me a fucking heart attack. Man! I ain't got no parachute. Talk about getting the adrenaline flowing. Scared the shit out of me!" Bud recounted vividly.

Anyway this was only the half of it. Skip, up front, had a death grip on his seat. He was staring straight ahead, unaware of Bud's predicament in the rear. He probably thought he'd fall out or something, and here Bud was, halfway gone. Now that Bud was so far out of the cockpit, he couldn't reach the controls. He damn sure couldn't reach the rudder pedals.

Bud continued, "Here we were, at three thousand feet altitude, upside down, pilot half in half out of the plane and flopping around like a rag in the wind. This and, you guessed it, ain't nobody flying shit!"

Bud thought for a second or two on how he was going to get back in the plane. They only thing he could come up with was to slide down and squeeze through the harness and lap belt until his armpits were about where the lap belt was. If he could get to the stick, he would roll back over to the upright position and make the necessary adjustments to the seat. After quite an effort, he finally got down in the seat far enough to pull the stick back with his foot and grab it with his hands. Problem number 2, as Bud recounted, started right then and there. In normal flight, if you pull back on the control stick, you climb or pitch up. Since they were inverted, the plane dove to the ground and upside down. Bud said he was starting to get really pissed.

"All right already, this shit can stop anytime now, kings X, I give," Bud said he murmured other things also. Now that the plane was headed down, Bud has to work fast. He finally got control back, rolled the plane over to upright, and since the control stick was in the pulled back position, it did about four G's and noses back up. With this added force, the seat, which up till now was in the fully extended position, let loose again. This time, it slammed down hard. Now it was full down. The loud bang that accompanied this event got Skip's attention. Skip turned around fast to see what Bud was up to. Imagine the look on Skip's face when he couldn't see Bud. Bud, being short, along with being slipped so far down in the seat and harness, had now put him below the visible level of the fuselage. Skip thought Bud had fallen out of the plane during the roll. He screamed in horror. Skip was terrified.

Bud said, "Damnedest thing, all of a sudden, there was this screaming up front. I thought, now what? Maybe a fucking bird hit him or something."

Skip, assuming Bud had parted company, realized that he would have to land the plane. Skip didn't know diddly squat about flying an airplane, much less a Stearman. However, he thought it was a life-or-death situation, and he was going down and land one way or another. Skip grabbed the stick, and to his great surprise, it wouldn't move. He tried over and over again. Nothing, very little at the most. There was a good reason too. Bud had it in the rear. Skip wouldn't let go. He banged it all around forcefully. Bud, being scrunched down with the stick up tight in his groin, wasn't happy. After a while, Bud got the seat back up to where it was supposed to be and reduced power. Skip hearing the engine power slow, turned around, and lo and behold, Bud's back. The expression on Skip's face was that of disbelief. Later Bud recalled, "If I only had a camera! It was one of those Norman Rockwell picture situations, serious but getting funnier by the moment."

The landing was uneventful. Later, everybody laughed about the whole ordeal.

That morning, Jim had come out to Potomac at Bud's request. Jim fixed the seat. Now they just sat in the office reminiscing about good times and great times. Jim had listened to the whole seat affair, and Bud swore that if he didn't know better, Jim had set him up. After a good while, Jim got up to go. They went outside. It was a beautiful day. Not a cloud in the sky. Bud and Jim looked at each other. Without saying a word, they were thinking the same thing. *Come on, take it up one more time.* Silent, still not saying a word, and then both at the same time said, "Naw, next time."

They laughed. It was going to get dark soon. Jim had an early flight tomorrow.

"Well, see you around the world someplace, Bud," Jim said.

"Hey, man! Watch your back! If you get back up this way anytime soon, you know where to find me," Bud replied.

Jim ended it up with just a "Later, dude!" and he drove off.

Bud thought to himself as Jim drove across the runway and up the hill, *What a guy.* Bud, Jim, Skip, Al, Colonel Moran—they were all that type of guy, the kind that just did it, the kind that loved in the fast lane, lived right, and were always there for the long haul, but then again, that's what being "American" is all about.

Panama City

The plane banked slowly as it approached Tocumen Airport. It was now called Omar Torrijos International Airport, but it was still Tocumen to Jim. He had flown in and out of it many times over the past years. This was just one more time. Rosa and the kids had just been there a few months earlier. Straining to see some recognizable landmark, Jim had his face pressed against the window. It was dark, and all the lights of Panama City were hypnotizing. The plane taxied to a stop, and everyone was getting prepared to get off and go their respective destinations.

"Well, this is it. We're here. Wonder what's in store for us?" Jim said.

He had filled out the tourist cards that the plane crew had passed around just after takeoff in Miami. After a short walk down the corridor connecting the plane to the terminal, they got in line to go through customs. Jim eyed everything. He tried to pick out any possible problem that might come up. That way, he could avoid it and not call any undue attention to himself or his family. Everything was going along pretty smoothly. Rosa was in the line first, then the children. Jim brought up the rear. The glass booth that held the immigration and customs officers was just ahead.

"Passports please," the man said. Rosa handed hers and the kids' passports to him. Jim slid up also, just as the officer started looking at the others.

"What's the nature of your visit?" he asked.

The guy looked mean. He looked at the documents, then looked up slowly, first at Jim and then Rosa.

"Visiting relative," Rosa said.

After a long questioning stare that had "why don't I believe you" written all over it, he said, "Okay, bueno." *Pow, Pow,* he stamped entry stamps with force that bordered on excess. He slid the passports to Rosa. He looked at Jim as he raised an eyebrow. Taking Jim's passport, he produced a large magnifying glass. Jim looked bewildered.

Rosa said to the guy firmly, "He's with me. He's my husband."

The guy with the stamp hesitated. The other official, the mean-looking one, said it was all right, "Let him pass. Just another tourist."

Then all of a sudden, out of nowhere, this guy pops up with a folded paper and hands it to the mean-looking immigration dude. He looks at it and then stops Jim with a moderately loud "alto!"

Uh-oh! Jim was confused. The guy that had handed the mean-looking officer the papers turned to Jim and called out, "Hi! I'm Joe Smith, from Evergreen. That's your orders from SOUTHCOM authorizing you and your family to get in. Shouldn't be but a minute."

Jim looked at him as to say, do what?

"Damn!" Jim said under his breath. "Man, I can't believe this shit!"

Now the official was pissed. The air was thick. With unquestionable seriousness, he demanded to know why Jim had lied and said he was visiting relatives when in reality, he was there to work for the "imperialist gringo pigs." Jim said nothing. Jim knew not to open his mouth in a situation such as this. Don't explain anything. Don't make excuses. Don't lie. He just stood there looking stupid.

"We'll have to get this approved." With that, the immigration officer left with Jim's passport. Jim didn't move an inch. The mean-looking dude was burning holes in Jim with his eyes.

Jim looked over at Joe. Joe waved and smiled. If only Joe had known what Jim was thinking. Jim was thinking, *As soon as I get past this rope, I'm going to kick the shit out of you, you ignorant son of a bitch.*

Jim operated very well on his own. He was well versed in procedures and methods that he had learned from flying in and out of backwoods, gee-dunk countries, and banana republics all over the world. Low profile nonhostile, nothing out the ordinary, able to be just one of the crowd—that was the ticket. Now it's been complicated. Enter the unexpected. Here's this guy bouncing all over the place, drawing attention. Jim kinda expected him to jerk out an American flag and start singing. Jim was definitely not a happy camper. Jim was still standing there. His wife and kids were on the other side of the turnstile. They looked concerned but not like this was happening in East Germany or something. After all, this was Panama, and Jim's wife was a Panamanian.

She also had some connections. Some of her relatives had been high-ranking officers in the La Guardia National. Her mother's second cousin was Colonel Flores, once a top-ranking officer under General Omar Torrijos. When Rosa was younger, she lived on Volcán Barú, a large volcano located in the province of Chiriquí, the largest province and most northern province in Panama. While there, Rosa worked for Torrijos at his home in Cerro Punta. Rosa used to watch over his son on occasion. Torrijos was just a lieutenant stationed at the David garrison at the time. After a term of employment with Torrijos, Rosa went to Panama City, where she attended the Instituto Nacional de Comercio. After graduating, she again worked for Torrijos as his son had asked for her.

Torrijos had just launched a major coup and had overthrown Arnulfo Arias, then president of the republic. Now he was a general and commander of the national guard. Since the republic was now under military law, he was now head of state. Rosa was then working for Manuel Jose Sedano, a world-renowned and much sought-after artist who had once taught at the University of Chicago, Illinois. He was famous for his presidential portraits. After Jim and Rosa got married, they would go up to her family' place in Batun, Bugaba. Rosas's family were the largest landowners in the area and were pretty well off.

On several occasions back in 1975, Jim would recount how they would go up to Torrijos's home in Cerro Punta and pick flowers. Rosa was still on good terms with Torrijos's relatives, although Omar Torrijos didn't stay there as much as he used to. Later on in his life, Torrijos had died in a freak helicopter crash. Noriega was now the man. Noriega had assumed the position of Commander de Fuerzas Armadas that Torrijos once held. Two completely different type of individuals. There was always that unanswered question of, did Noriega have anything to do with the crash? Jim had his opinion but kept it to himself.

Jim just kept standing there waiting. He wasn't that much worried. He should have been, though. Within a short period of time, the official came back and motioned for Jim to come forward. Jim nodded to Rosa to ease up to where he was headed. They both got to the glass booth at the same time. The guy just slid the passport through the hole in the bottom of the glass. Rosa was standing next to Jim. The official looked at Rosa first and shifted his gaze to Jim. In a low voice, he said, "Cuidar, Senor."

Jim looked puzzled. The officer removed his hand from covering the passport.

Rosa said, "Si, gracias."

Jim didn't say a word. He hadn't forgotten about this Joe character either. Jim took a quick look around but couldn't see Joe anywhere. Rosa told him that Joe had gone to bring the van around. He had just left with a another guy that had gotten off the plane with them. They now were standing there waiting for the luggage. Jim was sweating profusely. He was also getting impatient.

"Too many damn people in here. I gotta get out of this place," he said. "Oh, by the way, what did that dip shit mean by *cuidar*? Be careful of what?"

"I think it was more like watch out or maybe use caution," Rosa told Jim.

Jim figured it was like, "Okay, you can pass this time, but next time your butt is mine."

The well-traveled luggage arrived, and they all exited the terminal. Jim located the van. He put the bags in the back. It was good and dark by now, and it was still hot. As Jim and his family got in, they noticed for the first time this other guy that had been on the plane with them. He was sitting in the shotgun position up front. After Joe had pulled out on the main road to the city, he turned around and introduced himself.

"I'm Don Davis, the site manager down here. Welcome aboard."

Jim introduced his wife and kids.

"Glad to meet you," he said. "You know, it's not really that bad down here. The Panamanian people are real nice. You'll get used to it. It's sorta like the Philippines."

Philippines! Shit, this guy thinks my wife is a Filipino! I sure hope this whole deal ain't full of a bunch dumb shits. This guy doesn't have a clue. Jim's mind was racing.

"We've got a hotel set up down here. It's right off Punta Patilla and just down from the Patilla Airport. It's called the Caracol, on Avenida Brasil."

Jim knew it. It was a residencia in the affluent area of town.

"We'll be there soon, and you can get settled in," Davis said. He sounded almost proud.

"Settled in! You watch, probably got a big American flag hanging off the side or something," Jim mumbled to Rosa, low so only she could hear him. She gave Jim a pinch on the leg and a stern look. Jim knew what that meant.

"Uh, excuse me, but if it's all the same to you, just drop us off at the Hotel Continental. It's on the—"

Davis cut him off. "No, no, no, wouldn't hear of it. We've got you all set up. Everybody's there. You'll like it." Davis sounded off.

Rosa's look didn't change. Jim didn't like this at all. The last time someone set it all up like this was the Hotel Tynali, Islamabad, Pakistan. Everybody got dysentery. He was just going to have to go along, at least for a while. While Joe briefed Davis on what had been going on at the job, Jim and family just rode along in the back. As the van topped a small hill on the outskirts of Panama City, Andrew, Jim's son, blurts out, "Hey, Mom, there's Tia's house!"

He got David's attention. Now he was curious. Davis asked what he was pointing at. Jim told him that Andrew was pointing out his aunt's house. Davis, somewhat amused, and with a chuckle said, "Oh no, son, your mistaken, we're in Panama now. All those lights just look like the States."

Before Andrew could say a word, Mom was on him like a spider on a bug. "Sit down, shush!"

"But, Mom, that's really—"

"I said sit down," Rosa cut him off real quick.

Jim was about to bust. Su, Jim's daughter, who was always delighted when her younger brother got into trouble was smirking also.

Finally, after some time and a roundabout way, they arrived at the Caracol Hotel. As expected, was set up. They picked up the keys to the third floor and they all went up. Evergreen had rented a couple of floors, and as far as Jim could determine, the whole operation lived there. It was actually a residencia or residential hotel. More like an apartment complex than a Holiday Inn. In security terms, it was a nightmare. Jim spotted it right off. Later on everyone would find out just how big a nightmare it would be. Open outside walkways to the rooms, no lobby security, emergency stairwells open and unlocked could be accessed from the street, open access to first floor through the parking area, which also opened to the street, minimal lightning. It was the typical beach-type building, the kind Jim had seen all over the world: the Four Seasons just down the block from Bobby's in Athens; the Apollon, a little further down in the same area; Hessins in Messina, Sicily; Hotel Betolini in Palermo; or the Korat Hotel in Korat, Thailand—the list goes on. There, like so many others, made famous by the terrorists who blew them up. Jim had been there, done that. He wasn't partial to hanging his ass out or putting his family in a position to be taken advantage of.

"Now this is what I call a hotel," Jim told Joe, who apparently was on his first sojourn out of the good ole USA

"They ain't got nothing like this in Tel Aviv," Jim said.

"No kidding," Joe said as he was helping with the bags. Joe didn't have any idea that Jim was setting him up. Jim had decided not to kick his ass but instead had decided to make him look foolish. Jim was good, Joe was gullible.

"Well, actually they used to but not anymore," Jim told Joe as he pushed a suitcase with his foot.

"Oh yeah, why not?" Joe answered.

Jim turned around. He was on the room side of the door, and Joe was standing in the hall. Jim looked him straight in the eye. His hand was on the door.

"'Cause they blew the motherfuckers all up!"

Blam, the door slams shut.

"Damn it, damn it!" Jim exclaimed.

"What's the matter, viejo?" Rosa asked. She thought he had gotten his finger caught in the door.

"No peephole," how am I supposed to see that stupid look on his face if there ain't no peephole? Good thing the boss was in the van or he would be walking back from San Miguelito right now."

It had been a long day, and they were beat. The kids were watching TV, and Rosa had already hung up the clothes so they wouldn't wrinkle. Jim could hear faint music coming from outside. It brought back memories of twenty years ago, back to a time when Jim and Rosa were younger. They'd probably be out dancing somewhere right now. Ah, the good ole days. Jim let his mind drift. After a quick shower, they hit the sack. Tomorrow Jim would get processed in out at Howard AFB.

He knew the procedure. He had done it many times before, and it would be the same this time. He would go over to the contract office and fill out the papers. Then over to PSID (Pass and ID) for a card. Of course, it would be GS-11 or GS-12E and mission essential employee stamped, for sure. Then get a local driver's license. Once that was done, he would go out to the job site for whatever briefings were scheduled.

Jim knew he would be briefed by NIS due to the fact that he carried a secret clearance and now in country, an upgrade to top secret was in order. Howard AFB was just about the largest American Air Force Base this far south. Being such, everybody who was anybody had operations out of there. The army was working out of hangar one. Hangar two was contractors. Beech AeroSpace Services Inc. Lockheed was there also. In the middle part of the hangar area was a roped-off area were the TR-1s were kept under armed guard. The TR-1 was a high-altitude, intelligence-gathering type of aircraft also known as the U-2. Used by the military intelligence community, information it provided was also shared by the different agencies that had operations down south, including the DEA. Hangar three contained GLASCO, Gates Lear Aircraft Services Company, who provided the C-21 Learjet attached to SOUTHCOM for use by the embassy. E-Systems was also there, as well as Boeing. Evergreen Helicopters Inc. had their own building built down at the extreme end of runway 24 to maintain a low-profile, out-of-sight status. If everything went along well, Jim would get mostly done in one day.

Later on in the afternoon, he would go by the NCO Club when he had time. Jim figured he would stop by the club, have a couple of beers with the guys, and then on the way back to town, stop by Rodman Naval Station and rent a car. Jim wasn't going to ride around in the van with everybody else and be tied down to the blue route or secure route laid out by SOUTHCOM. He sure wasn't up to sitting around waiting for the van to come back from dropping off the pilots and take him to the hotel. After getting off work, it was time to split. Waiting on Joe to show up wasn't going to cut it. So far, everything was going okay. He knew it would take a week or so to get settled into the routine. For Jim, time was of the essence. This week would go fast, and the first thing on the agenda was to put some distance between himself and the regular pattern. Jim remembered what Colonel Moran had told him in Washington. From experience, Jim knew that complacency and repetition could get you in trouble real fast. Irregular movement and unpredictably were your allies. It's hard to get a fix on an erratic target. If you vary your route and times, it makes it difficult to predict where and when you will show. To Jim, it was like being stuck way out on a limb.

The same routine, day in and day out, was just asking for trouble. In the morning, he would take care of business and start making arrangements to become less dependent on someone else. If everything went as planned, he'd be completely on his own by week's end.

It was way past midnight when they got to sleep. The 0500 wake-up call in the morning was just hours away. Little did he know that wasn't the only thing just hours away. Operation Just Cause was well into the planning stages. The final times and dates were being set. It was now just a matter of time.

Evergreen CASA 212 Aircraft

Evergreen CASA 212 Aircraft

Panama Defense Forces Comandancia

Panama Defense Forces Comandancia

Back area of PDF Comandancia

Comandancia back lot

Apartment quarter behind comandancia

Panama Defense Forces Barracks

PDF compound area destroyed by U.S. Army

Carcel Modelo (prison) where Kurt Muze was held prisoner

G-3 Intelligence Office

Panama Defense Forces barracks destroyed during
Operation "Just Cause", Panama City

PDF detention cell block

PDF detention cell block

PDF offices, Special Forces

Destroyed PDF transport vehicles

Damages from U.S. Forces "Just Cause", Panama City

Author in front of damaged city area

Barber shop, Comandancia

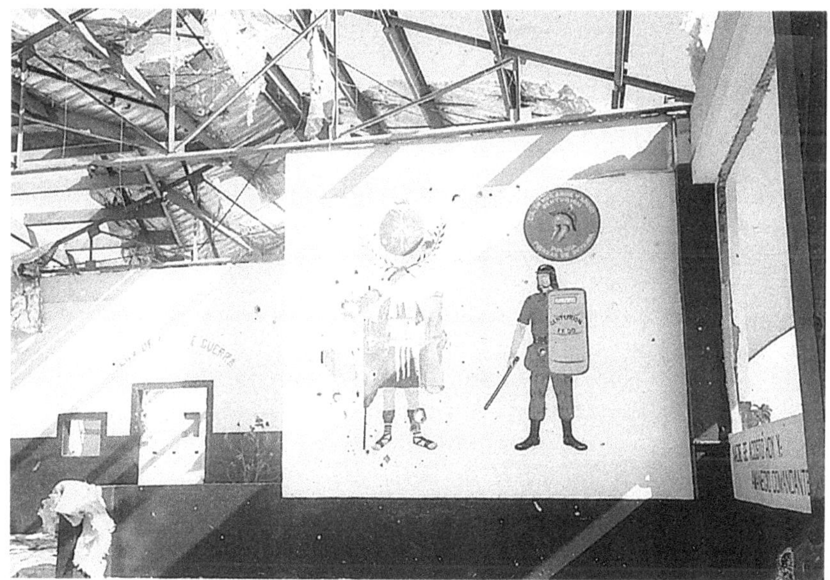

Comandancia wall art

PDF Unit / command symbols

PDF Unit / command symbols

CHAPTER 10

Getting Settled

The morning came fast. Still sleepy from lack of it, Jim had showered and was out on the open air walkway, waiting for the van to get back from Howard. Joe had taken the aircrews in for the early morning launch and was on his way back to pick up the remaining personnel. Joe finally showed up, and the rest of the guys loaded up and took off. By now, traffic wasn't bad. They arrived at the Evergreen facility within the hour. After they all got inside where the air conditioner was already straining, Jim reported in to Don Davis. Don was just getting off the phone, and as Jim stood there, he thought to himself that Davis looked familiar. Jim couldn't place him, but he felt that their paths had crossed somewhere before.

Davis introduced Jim to Doug Beatty. Doug was the maintenance supervisor there at Howard. He had been with Evergreen for around ten years. Doug had worked on programs from Alaska to Peru. Doug was married, and his wife was from El Salvador. Doug's wife, Esparanza, and Jim's wife would surely get along.

As for the other employees, most were single or had left their families in the States. Unless you were used to overseas life, with the hardships that come with it, then it probably would be a good idea to not bring them with you. Jim had seen this many times before. A guy would show up in some less than nice, hostile backwoods site with wife in tow. A couple of weeks later, Jim would be calling a replacement. Doug stuck out his hand, and they shook. Doug had Jim's paperwork in hand.

"Been expecting you. Rick Ketchum said you come highly recommended. I've just got one question for you. Seems every place you've been in the past ten years, there's been some sort of conflict going on. Let's see, Turkey, Pakistan, the Argan war, right! El Salvador, Germany, Greece, Chad, Sicily for three years. Libyan crisis, I presume. A year in Washington, DC, out at Andrews. I don't even want to know about that. And now here we are in Panama?"

"Well yeah, you left out a couple of spots in South East Asia and Africa, but that's about right. DC sucks! Got kinda slow, so I had to go," Jim told Doug with a smile.

"Well, you got the next two days off to take care of whatever it is you have to do. I know you can handle it," Doug said.

He was smiling also. *Not a problem*, Jim thought to himself.

The next couple of days, he did just that. Jim rented a car from Budget over at Rodman, got his family ID cards and after taking care of what it was he had to do, rented a house on the far side of Veracruz. Veracruz was a small fishing town just out the back gate on Fort Kobbe and down a short ways from Venado Beach. The place that Jim rented belonged to a major in the PDF (Panamanian Defense Force). He was pro-American and had been involved in a failed coup attempt to remove Noriega. Now he was doing hard time with torture at the local big-time prison at Gamboa, compliments of the general himself. Since he wouldn't be needing the house for a while, and his family could use the income that he no longer could provide, his mother agreed to rent it out for him. The house was nice. It came with swimming pool, palm trees, and a covered picnic area poolside. A tall white wall surrounded the whole complex. It had large double swinging front gates of iron. Above the gates was a large brass bell that could be rung from the outside to signal those inside that they had visitors and someone should come down to the gate and let them in. It looked like the entrance to a presidio. The yard was dotted with coconut palms and local flora. There were spots of flor de verano, palo santo and bird-of-paradise. In the back, there was papaya, yucca, and plantain. The walls were topped with broken glass, a custom in central American countries. It kept people from climbing over, to a certain extent.

Jim had also made arrangements with one of the mechanics to purchase his car. He had some problems with the locals breaking into his place and decided to go up to Soto Cano Air Base, Honduras, as permanent party. Evergreen had a sister site up there and had access to on base quarters for their personnel. On-base housing was not available to contractors in Panama due to the treaty agreement that Carter and Torrijos had signed back in 1979. Dave "the Dude" had told Jim that when he left he would sell him the car for five hundred dollars and a meal.

Dave figured Soto Cano would be safer for him and was looking forward to leaving. Soto Cano was a strange place. It used to be called Palmerola Air Field, but the name was changed after a change of command and was renamed after General Soto Cano.

Comayagua was the closest town and a place that Jim would get familiar with latter on.

By now, Jim had taken care of most everything, and it looked like it would be nothing but "job" starting in the morning. The total amount of time it took to set up was four days. Jim used to say that he could go anyplace in the world, set up living arrangements, and be fully operational within five days, including travel time. The next two weeks or so, things were pretty much the same. Evergreen was making several missions a day. Usually they came in and launched the aircraft out at first light. Late shift would come in and recover the aircraft in the evening. Sometimes, if a plane came back broke, the late shift would have stay and fix it. Most of the time, the planes were back from Honduras, and they would have a spare plane available. Spares were available in case one was broke and needed a part to be ordered. In all, the operation was running along smoothly.

Downtown Panama City was different story. It was real tense. Military patrols were everywhere. There were off-and-on demonstrations around the university. There were confrontations on Central Avenue. The newspapers covered storied of pro-Noriega troops beating Panamanian civilians. There were front-page photos of a bloody vice president Ford running for his life with Dignity Battalion thugs in hot pursuit. The elected president Endara could not take office. He had been exiled to Miami shortly after the last elections. The

Dignity Battalion troops, dressed in civilian clothes, would show up out of nowhere. They beat the protesters. They beat people for public assembly. They would show up, do the damage, and disappear in a wisp. At night, it was worse. Every day and especially at night, people would disappear. Sometimes they were found dead days later and miles from the city. Sometimes never found.

They would come at night and take you away for questioning. You never reappear. Next day, next week, nobody knows nothing. The Panamanians would still talk about Dr. Spadafora, the doctor who fought for liberty and spoke out a little too much. They found his headless corpse just across the Costa Rican border along a place they call "La frontera." Jim knew exactly where it was. Rosa was from the area. Back in 1974, they used to go dancing at Conception, where typical music was played by Yin Carrizo, Ayala, and Cardenas nightly. This was where Jim had met Mr. Johnson, an American who had a nice place on a private lake a couple of klicks outside of Volcan. The oppression wasn't as great up north as it was in the city, but it was still present. You had to watch what you said and who you were seen with.

Over the next few weeks or so, confrontations escalated in Panama City. Noriega disbanded the congress. He declared himself supreme ruler and dictator of the republic. He ordered hostile actions against American civilians as well as a shoot-on-sight order on any US Military personnel found within the borders of Panama. On television, he was shown waving a machete and demanding all US forces withdraw from the region immediately. Shots were being fired at night. Screams were heard down alleys and bodies found in the morning. Then several PDF troops fired on a carload of marine officers.

And if that wasn't enough, an enlisted navy petty officer and his wife were assaulted and beat. Jim had been going to and from work without incident all these days. Probably because he didn't live downtown and partly due to the low profile he liked to keep. This particular day, he was going out the Fort Kobbe back gate and had the radio on, listening to the news. He sometimes listened to a Panamanian station to get a more detailed report on what the situation was in the city. Today Noriega was being carried live, and he was really letting the USA have it. His speech was being broadcast countrywide as he was addressing the national assembly. He used all the usual slanders and lies. He was giving it all his worth today, Jim thought. Then Noriega made a big mistake. Jim couldn't believe what he was saying. Noriega started referring to the present situation between the United States and Panama as being close to a state of war. He, in effect, was giving the go-ahead for severe preemptive strikes against US citizens residing in the interior of the Republic of Panama. If bodies started turning up, the blood would not be on his hands but on the hands of the imperialists. Jim just kept on driving through Veracruz to his house on the far side.

Man, this is some heavy shit, he thought to himself.

"State of war! Yeah, right. It's the 17th of December! It's too close to Christmas to start a war. Besides, all my neat wartime equipment isn't here yet. Damn that Military Postal Service sucks." Jim had noticed a little extra activity on the field, but up till now, just another day, 'nother dollar.

CHAPTER 11

The Buildup, 18th and 19th

Today was December 18, a Monday, and for some reason, Evergreen had no assigned missions for the day. Of course, anything can change at any time. Yesterday Jim and a couple of the mechanics had come in and launched out the replacement aircraft to Soto Cano. The normal rotation was around every couple of weeks. The aircrafts rotated back as well. Jim had noticed that the amount of activity and air traffic Sunday was unusual, and today, it seemed the military was quite busy again. There was some talk and Mr. Davis speculated that a major force re-allocation to Panama was underway. That morning there wasn't much going on other than catching up on paperwork and polishing the tools. Ken Seaman called from McMinnville, Oregon, and talked with Mr. Dickinson. Mr. Dickinson was the senior pilot and aircrew operations manager for the Casa Program. At the time nobody knew what the call was about, but later it was learned what one of the pilots was being sent back to the states. The rest of the morning, Davis and Dickson were busy with out-processing of the pilot, Mr. Miller. Since the out-processing would take a day or more, it would have to take a backseat to the other concerns that were becoming more and more apparent with each passing hour. Mr. Dickinson was responsible for the pilots, so he would be taking care of the most of the arrangements. This left Davis to inquire as to what was going on. He had concerns that he needed to voice.

That afternoon, Davis met with Mrs. Black, the ACO. He informed her of his concerns relative to the ongoing build up at Howard. Davis requested base housing to be provided for Evergreen personnel. That is, if there was anything planned that he needed to know about to ensure operational integrity. She indicated to him that base housing was not available to civilian personnel as specified in the contract. She, however, did explain that SOUTHCOM was looking at alternatives for contractor quarters. Davis related to Mrs. Black that he feared for the security of Evergreen personnel who live in Panama City. He asked if it would help matters if he wrote a letter to command. He also expressed additional concerns that would affect logistics. If Evergreen was to continue to be considered a flyable asset, then in the event of a major operational effort, the employees might not be able to make the trip in the town. If hostilities continued to escalate, there might a problem since over half the route taken every day was not on the "designated" SOUTHCOM secure routes map. Jim has spotted this problem right off. He had informed Doug about it and then moved. Nothing was ever done about it. Mrs. Black told Davis that she would discuss the matter with Mr. Hammond. Mr. Hammond was the contracting officer at Headquarters MAC. Back at the Evergreen office, Jim was getting ready to head for the house. Karson Branham, one of the original hire mechanics, was waiting for Joe to get back from picking up Davis over at the 61ˢᵗ MAG. He had gone over there to see if he could drum up some support on his request for base housing. Karson was going home to the states for the holidays and was needing a ride out to the airport. Little did he know that he would get out just under the wire.

"Hey, Doug! Dollar waitin' on a dime, dude! If we're going to do it, then let's do it!" Jim yelled from back in the shop. Everybody had already cut out since it was a down day. Only Jim and Doug were left in the shop. Joe, Davis, and Karson had taken off in the van and were probably across the bridge by now. Doug finished up, and the both of them locked up and headed for the NCO Club.

"What do you make of all the increased activity?" Jim said as they walked out to the parking lot.

"Beats me," Doug replied. "Maybe they'll let us in on the secret tomorrow. I know one thing, though, I ain't seen nothing like this in a long time. Know what I mean?"

Jim looked at Doug. He knew exactly what he meant. As they drove past tall palm trees and freshly cut grass, Jim said, "You know it won't be like this tomorrow."

"Oh yeah," Doug replied. "Why's that?"

'Well, it wasn't like this yesterday, was it?" Jim smiled.

Doug just shook his head and smiled also.

"Oh, by the way, a guy called for you earlier today. Said he was a friend of yours and asked me to pass a message." Doug fumbled in his pocket for the note. "Said his name was Moran or something like that."

"Yeah, Moran, I know him. What did he want?" Jim was anxious.

"Well, I can't find that paper, but all he said was that he was going to drop by in a couple of days, so don't go too far away from the house. Said you would know what he meant." Doug figured something was up, and Jim probably has a good idea what.

Today, Tuesday, came early. It started out like any other. Jim had gotten up around 0500, eaten breakfast, and driven down through Veracruz and over to Doug's house. It was cool with a slight breeze coming in off the Pacific Ocean but not that cool. Veracruz, being right on the water, always had a cool morning breeze. Jim parked out on the street and was inside when the phone rang. After a short conversation, Doug appeared and said, "Let's go. That was Davis out at the base. Said if he's got to be there early, then we've got to be there early!"

"Early! Shit, it's six o'clock," Jim remarked. Doug kissed his wife, Esparanza, goodbye, and out they headed to work. The ride into Howard was uneventful. As Jim drove up to the back gate, nothing seem unusual. As they drove around the runway perimeter and into Fort Kobbe, the scenery began to change. Off to the right on a big grassy area and all the way back to the tree line were large canvas tents, portable buildings, latrines, and all the other associated equipment that accompanied a large troop movement. This was definitely a support unit of sorts. On the left were any number of helicopters.

Some arranged in rows, others in random placement, some running ready to takeoff. There were Apaches, Blackhawks, Loaches,

Hueys, and ground crews on headsets everywhere. In the larger area further down, Doug spotted more aircraft. Doug had a passion for helicopters. Had it ever since Vietnam. Doug, on occasion, when he was out with Jim, would relate stories of operations he had been a part of over there. Jim could relate.

"Man! Where'd all this shit came from?" Jim spoke, somewhat surprised.

Doug took a forced look around and said, "Hmm, looks like they're from the states. What do you think?" Dough like to catch Jim off guard like that.

Jim, with a quick answer, "Yeah! Oh look, Doug, there's an American flag on that one! Never a dull moment around here. I wonder how long they're in town for?"

By now, they both were laughing. Jim just kept on driving onto Howard. Things on Howard were a mess, to say the least. The ramp area was packed with C-130s, C-141s, C-5s, and a whole bunch of other transports, gunships, and people. Aircraft were landing as others were taking off. At any one time, they could count a dozen or more in the pattern over and around the field. Hangar One, Two, Three were packed with troops and equipment. Hundreds of combat-ready airborne were assembled. 101st airborne, 82nd Airborne and special operations units were geared up and strung out all over the place. It looked ominous, to say the least. Out front of Hangar Three were five or six Spectre gunships. They are C-130s with Vulcan cannons that rain death from above. The Grim Reaper and Skeleton painted Special Air Operations Symbols left no doubt who they were. Anyone who was ever seen these birds in action would never forget it. The weird buzz and whirling sounds accompanied by beams of light emitted by thousands of tracers streaming down and impacting the ground in seconds left no doubt that death from above was a good analogy of just what these guys could deliver.

True or not, it was said that one Spectre could put a round in every square inch of a football field in seconds. If true, that's awesome. Last night thousands of soldiers had landed at Howard AFB. Hundreds of aircraft of various shapes, sizes, and origins now dotted the tarmac. The tension was so thick, you could see it, smell it, feel it. Goose bumps, dormant for a long time, now appeared at each new encounter as they drove slowly and silently along the perimeter fence. Doug and Jim were not ready for this. They both knew what was going on.

They didn't have to say a word. It came from being there, from experience. It came from being shot at and missed, shit at and hit! Now, suddenly it wasn't funny anymore. It was a situation that was sensed. A slap in the face. Low-grade adrenaline rush that made the hair on the back of your neck stand up. It was sort like knowing someone was sneaking up on you from behind and turning quickly catching them in the act.

Arriving at the parking lot across from the MAC Terminal, Jim parked, and they went inside through the controlled access entry point. The shop was all the way at the end of the ramp. As they approached the Evergreen building, they noticed that a MASH unit had set up on the grass area directly in front. That clinched it. This was not some exercise, as some had hinted it was.

"Christ! That's no first-aid station there. That's a full grown army hospital unit!" Jim exclaimed.

Doug didn't say a word. He looked pissed off. Jim was still unsure. If it was saber-rattling, the US was sure giving it a good show. If not, well, they'd soon find out. Davis, Dickson and "driver Joe" were in the office. Dickson was staring out the front windows. He did this all the time. Davis was on the phone. Joe was in the head taking a crap. Davis hung up the phone and told Joe, who was coming back up front, to get the guys at the Caracol, all of them, and get back there ASAP.

"Hey, Doug, that was Major Tucker at the 61st MAG. Said he wanted us to move the aircraft to another location on the field. He didn't know where yet, but LTC Lanier would allocate us a spot later this morning. Said to stand by." Davis sounded concerned. He looked dazed. He was speaking, but his mind was a million miles away.

"Oh, and tow them. Don't taxi them over. Run over some grunt out here and I'll never hear the end of it," he added.

There were only three planes at Howard. The rest were up in Honduras. Doug finished smoking his cigarette and went outside to where Jim was.

"Jim, let's go down to the 61st MAG and see where LTC Lanier wants us to put the birds."

Jim and Doug jumped on the Coleman tug and headed down to Hangar One an Hangar Two. They were to put them on the ramp and up against the fence. Then, if available, cover them with camouflage netting. There they would be out of the way and somewhat hidden. LTC Lanier didn't give them any reason for the move; it was just understood. The time duration would be for one or two days.

That afternoon, Davis made several more attempts to get additional information from the 61st MAG as to what the game plan was. Davis spoke with LTC Burns, Major Tucker, LTC Lanier, and Captain McGillvary. None of them were willing to provide any additional information to Evergreen as to what was officially under way. It was obvious, but was it imminent. Davis wanted to have it in writing. If that was not possible, at least get it from the proverbial horse's mouth. This obsession to be in on the deal and have all the information on what was to transpire would be a major factor in making security decisions that would affect the bulk of Evergreen personnel. It was evident what was going on, and it was definitely not going down next week. It was now, and it was serious.

By the time Doug and Jim got back to Evergreen, Joe had returned from Panama City. All Evergreen personnel were on base and accounted for. The rest of the day, everybody found something to do. They kept busy, or at least looked busy. Around 1700 hours, Major Tucker called and asked Davis if he had made any further attempt to secure on base accommodations. Davis told him that he had contracted Mrs. Black several times, but she still had been noncommittal. Major Tucker told Davis he needed to do something, and it needed to be done that afternoon. Major Tucker called the contracting office to talk to Mrs. Black; however, she had already left for the day. Davis provided the major with her home phone number, and he called her at home. Time was running out, and the major was helping as best he could. Major Tucker got ahold of Mrs. Black and told her that Evergreen employees needed emergency temporary quarters, even if it was only a cot in a barracks. Mrs. Black, becoming agitated with this issue, told Major Tucker that she could not be any assistance in this matter and suggested that if he had any further questions regarding this situation, he not call her but call her supervisor, the chief of contract services. She gave the major the phone number. Major Tucker called and was promptly told that since it was after normal duty hours, nothing could be done and suggested that he come by the office tomorrow sometime, and they would discuss it.

The major was pretty pissed off. Evidently the contract office didn't have a clue. The whole deal was like beating a dead horse. Davis figured that since no one had told him what was in the works for tomorrow, then nothing was in the works for tomorrow. He would work on this lodging issue in the morning. Somewhere along the line, priorities were lost, and a severe breakdown in communications happened. Davis released everyone to go to their residences, if they so desired. Doug, Jim, and a couple of mechanics that also lived in the Veracruz area stayed late to relocate the aircraft after dark. Hopefully it wouldn't take too long, and they would at least be home by midnight. Once back downtown, Davis ate super and then sent Tom Eastman and Nick Stolman out to Torrijos Airport to pick up the replacement pilot, Bill McQuade. He would be replacing Jim Miller, who was due to leave on Friday. Bill arrived at 8:55 p.m., and all three got back to the Caracol around 1100 hours.

The guys out at the base were just finishing up. Davis set Bill up in the room 57. He was in the room next to Davis. After getting settled, they all turned in.

Jim and Doug drove up to the back gate on Fort Kobbe. The PML Condition Board reflected PML Delta. PML Charlie was a heightened condition of alert. PML Delta was no unnecessary travel, possible hostile conditions exist. Delta is critical, to say the least. The only thing worse would be PML Echo, which was hostile forces presently engaged in action. No one in, no one out. As Jim approached the security point, the MP stepped out and waved his arms. He motioned for Jim to pull over and stop.

"Now what!" Jim said.

"Where you guys going?" the MP replied.

"Home. Veracruz. Had all the fun I can stand for today." Jim was looking at the MP.

"Sir, we're on PML Delta, and any minute it will go to Echo. No one in, no one out." The MP was hot and cocked. He was young, and he looked nervous. "Sir, I can let you guys out, but I can't guarantee you will be able to get back on base. So be advised, sir."

Doug and Jim looked at each other. Jim looked at the MP.

"Can't get back on base, can't work on the planes. Besides if they want to fly, we've got the keys. Right, Doug?"

Doug leaned over. "What happens at midnight or so that we might want to know about?"

The MP, still in serious mode, said, "You guys mission-essential personnel? If so, I need ID cards to verify names, and I'm going to need a point of contact, a POC, also. That's so we can come find you in case we have to come get you out."

Jim and Doug handed over their ID cards. The MP took the names and addresses and went to call it in over the radio.

"Okay! You're good to go, sir. Oh, just in case no one has advised you, if it was me, I would make sure I had a weapon on hand."

He stepped back one step, saluted, and Jim drove through the last lighted area until he would pull into Veracruz. It was 11:30 p.m. Veracruz was just three klicks from the back gate. Doug's house was the first big white house on the right. It was a two-story place where the boulevard started. They passed by, and there were no lights on. Jim headed for the pizzeria. It was next to the mercado. It was a good place to get a couple of beers to relax and then Jim would take Doug back home. Then he would drive back through Veracruz to his place on the far side of town. Jim lived the farthest out, all the way to the bottom of the mountain and then right next to the jungle. He liked it that way. They sat at the bar drinking an Atlas draft.

"What do you make of this?" Jim asked. "With all this extra security, plus what's been going on today." Both of them knew that the shit was getting ready to hit the fan.

"I don't think anything will happen tonight, maybe after Christmas sometime," Doug answered.

"Yeah, you're probably right," agreed Jim.

"So what's the message from that dude Moran about?" Jim had already forgotten.

"He's a colonel I know up in DC Works out of the Pentagon now a days. I've known him for years. We go way back. Every now and then, we cross paths somewhere around the world. Defense attaché officer, liaison officer, special operations assignments here and there. He owes me a favor and has been trying to pay me back for a while. Sometimes I owe him. I think it's I owe him right now. Yesterday it was he owes me. Get the picture?"

Doug let it go at that. Jim should have taken the message a little more seriously.

Around midnight, the place was fixing to close so they bought one for the road.

"Dame dos cervezas para llavar, por favor," Jim asked the girls behind the bar. They got their cans and went out the front. Everything was quiet around that time, but it felt weird to them somehow. Jim dropped Doug off and turned around and went home. He got to the house around 12:30 a.m. and after a quick shower, hit the sack. The kids were asleep, and Rosa was doing the same. Jim slid into bed, beat. He let out a deep breath and drifted off.

December 20, 1989

"Jim! Jim! wake up." Rosa was shaking him softly. Jim suddenly sprang to life.

"What?" he answered, agitated.

"I think something's happening!" Rosa whispered.

"Do what?" He looked around in the dark, still groggy from being awakened from a deep sleep. "I don't hear anything. What time is it?"

Jim got up slowly and walked into the front room. He walked over to the front door. Pausing for just moment, he opened it and stepped outside. A cool light breeze was bowing. It smelled like ocean. At first, he noticed nothing, except there were quite a few lights on the surrounding houses. A long way off, he could hear muffled shouts or talking. He couldn't tell. There were some banging of pots together, and dogs were barking down in town. A strange glow was coming from the east. Something wasn't right. Rosa stood behind him. She strained to hear.

"They're saying…" She paused. She turned her head to catch the sounds. "The Americans are coming, The city's on fire. Invasion!" She turned white as the shouts became louder. "Invasion! Viejo! Get in here!" Rosa was very concerned.

Jim just stood there. A million things flashed through his mind—Andrews, Colonel Moran, tensions in Panama City, hostile actions against Americans, the build-up at Howard. A cold rush shivered through Jim. Quickly he turned, and Rosa saw the look on his face, a look of being caught with your pants down.

The sudden realization of being caught up in something that has taken you by surprise is uncomfortable, to say the least. Jim stepped to the door. Suddenly a very familiar sound of an attack helicopter broke the intermittent silence. It passed directly overhead and not more than a few feet above the palms. Jim jumped through the door and ducked. Then *swoosh, swoosh* in rapid succession, followed by a loud, deep *boom*. The windows rattled. There were flashes on the mountain where the rockets impacted. The mountain rose up from Veracruz and Chumical on the coast. It was called Punta Cabra. Mostly because it has twin peaks that resemble a goat's head. Inside the house, the kids were now up.

"Turn on the tube," Jim said, as he headed for the bedroom. Rosa told them to be quiet and get dressed. Jim was doing the same. The TV came on. However, it emitted nothing but static. Rosa flipped through the channels, but to no avail. Nothing was on. Andrew, Jim's son, turned on the radio. The same thing, not station one. Now dressed, Jim tried calling Doug. The phone was dead, not even a dial tone. They could hear automatic small weapons fire close by. An aerial flare popped. The outside was turned to a green glow. Silence. After a few minutes, the light went out, and the gunfire resumed. It was closer now. The neighbors were outside in back of their house and yelled over to Rosa. They told her the water was off. Since Jim had a tank that held five hundred gallons for those times the water pressure was low, they wanted to make sure we had plenty. Just in case they might need to borrow some. Another explosion shook the house.

Two more followed in quick succession. If there was any doubt about the situation, it was gone now. Jim wasn't worried about the water. That's why he had the storage tank. For the next couple of hours,   the small arms fire and occasional boom of something larger going off came and went. He took this time to assess the situation, inventory supplies, and weigh the operations. Jim was in the back room that he used for a secure area. He opened up a foot locker where he stocked the firepower. He called to Rosa, and when she came in, he handed her the Remington 1100 12-gauge and a bandolier of assorted 00 buck and no. 4 field loads in alternating order. Jim slid the 9mm Browning Hi-Power in his shoulder holster and stuck two loaded clips in his pants, one in each back pocket. He handed the ammo box to his daughter. It contained around one hundred twenty rounds of 9mil, a .25 cal. Titan automatic and some special 12-gauge rounds that Jim had mooched off some special forces dudes the week before. Jim told Rosa to watch the front, and he would watch the back. It was now just before daylight. The roosters were crowing. *How strange*, Jim thought, *roosters crowing to the complement of gunfire.* He smiled to himself as he remembered last night at the back gate when the MP suggested he might want to find a gun.

Su Yim, Jim's daughter, was peeking out the front windows. Suddenly she came running down the hall. "Oh my god! Oh my god! Mom! Mommmm! They're here. Oh my god! Dad! Mom! Come here! Quick!"

Rosa dropped what she was doing and ran to the front room. Jim was already there. Su Yim was shaken. Jim turned and spoke softly, "No English! If you have to talk, speak Spanish, or use hand signals. No lights! And turn off that stupid TV!"

Jim didn't want draw any attention to the fact that they were home. Outside the front wall and in the street, there was a big commotion going on. There about two dozen armed Panamanians in civilian clothes. They had bandanas over their faces. They were heavily armed with all sorts of weapons, including what looked like RPGs. Two or three of them were talking loudly and appeared to be almost arguing. Jim and Rosa peeked through the curtains in the living room.

"It's Mango, our neighbor," Rosa said. "The big guy wants to know where the Americans live. Mango's telling him we left for the base last night."

Jim was looking out in the predawn light. Suddenly he saw a head looking straight at him. Jim almost shit his pants. They stared at each other for almost a full minute. Suddenly the head dropped down behind the wall.

Jim's mind raced. *Did he see me? If he did, will he tell? Twenty to one, not great odds in a gun battle.*

Jim was wound tighter than a cheap watch. Suddenly someone yelled, and they scattered like a covey of quail. A few seconds passed, and an armored vehicle rolled by with the hammer down. US Army in hot pursuit of something or someone. Jim was glad to see there were at least some green uniforms in the area.

It continued like that all morning. Jim could smell rubber burning. Smoke, haze, and fog of the early morning made visibility low. He comforted his wife and kids, as they were definitely agitated. Around midday, he decided to walk down through town to Doug's house and see what he was up to. Rosa didn't like it worth a damn, In fact, she thought it pretty much a stupid idea. Jim told her to stay at the house with the kids, and if he wasn't back in two hours, to go out the back way and make her way to Fort Kobbe by way of the beach. She reluctantly agreed. Jim gave her a kiss and slipped out the back. He came up and around the outside wall. There was a path that went to the street from the back where some Kuna Indians lived. He poked his head out carefully and looked up and down the street. It looked good to go. Everything was unusually quiet. It could change at any moment, though. He was wearing a typical guayabera shirt, common in the tropics, and a panama hat. He had the 9mm stuck in his belt under his shirt. He had put four clips of ammo in his pockets, one clip in each. He figured that if someone saw him from a distance, he would look like a local. If someone got closer, he would pass as a "Zonie."

A "Zonie" was a term that was used to described white Canal Zone residents, part Panamanian and part American. Jim walked briskly into town. He passed the vacant hospital and didn't see anyone or anything. Across the bridge, he passed the soccer field. Behind it and up a ways was the Veracruz School. The place was always full of kids and adults having fun, playing checkers, talking or arguing about the last Roberto Durán fight. Not this day. It was vacant, and the only thing that moved was some plastic grocery bag blowing around in the wind and a mangy dog rummaging about for scraps of food as usual.

Now Jim approached the central part of town, and the scene began to change. The mercado building, pizzeria and pharmacy were totally gutted. Out front a car was completely burned and still smoldering. Up a little further were more fires. There were more burned cars on the side of the street. Some were upside down. Some were shot up real good. Some were only half there, the other half who knows where. Now Jim could see people running around here and there. They would run up to the house, bang on the door, shout something, then disappear inside. Women herded children along from this place to that, with clothes in plastic bags and carrying bottle water. The most peculiar thing was that there were old people, women, and small children out but no men. Jim guessed that either they were holed up someplace scared shitless or dead. Or maybe, he thought, they headed for the hills at the sound of the first shot.

Now almost all the way through town and to the far side, he entered the main town square. Store fronts were burned. The police garrison was vacant and dark inside. Jim could hear off in the distance someone crying or wailing, others shouted randomly. The front wall of the garrison was riddled with pockmarks from bullets. A large hole from what looked like a rocket still smoked. It looked bad, real bad. Jim passed by the taxi stop and crossed the last bridge that marked the edge of town. Doug's house was about half klick up on the left. Jim glanced at his watch. Walking out of town, Jim felt relief. Now the road was a boulevard.

There was a lot of space around. The beach was on the right, and the mountains were on the left. It still had patches of fog on the sides, and the top was covered with clouds. Looking up the coast toward Venado Beach, all the cabanas and bars look closed. Jim turned up the drive to Doug's house. Lobo, Doug's Doberman pincher, started barking.

"Hey, Doug! It's Jim, I'm coming in, so don't shoot me or something. Rosa would be really pissed if you messed up my shirt." He passed the corner.

"Around back," Doug yelled from inside. The house girl met Jim at the iron gate. "Buenos dias, Senor Jim. Como estas?"

"Bien, bueno," Jim responded.

Jim entered the house from the rear. Esparanza asked about Rosa. He told her everything was fine and tried not to look like anything was wrong. Jim played it off as just another day in a war zone. Jim really needed to talk to Doug. Doug was on the phone. He waved at Jim and motioned for him to come over and have a seat. Doug covered the phone with his hand and spoke to Jim.

"Man! You ain't gonna believe this shit! I've got McMinnville on the line, and they've got Washington on a conference line." Doug interrupts on the phone, "Look, dumbass, I don't care what the situation is with the fucking press. I'm telling you that the army was there, and they aren't. There's a lot of blood in most of the rooms. No! No American bodies. Yeah, Panamanian bodies. How the hell do I know. Maybe our guys took some of them out before they disappeared."

Jim looked bewildered. "Blood? Bodies? Sounds ominous to me, Doug. So what's the situation?" Doug set the phone down on the table and rubbed his forehead.

"I've got to keep an open line until they decide something. Your phone work?" Doug asked. "Tried call you but no good."

"Poles are all down in town. I ain't got shit. No electric, no water no nada," Jim replied.

"Well!" Doug paused. "Looks like we got wiped out last night. Everyone at the Caracol is gone."

"What do you mean gone?" Jim asked concerned.

"I mean gone! Like missing! Disappeared! Vanished! The army liaison said that the PDF stormed the apartment complex, and after the gunfire, took them all off somewhere. He said there's a lot of blood everywhere but no American bodies."

"So who's left?" Jim replied.

"Look like it's just you and me," Doug said as he picked the phone back up. Jim just sat there wondering what next. *Okay*, he thought himself. *Need to know exactly what the military situation is before making any decisions.* He got up and started for the door. "Be back in a few, Doug."

Doug put his hand over the phone. "Where you going?"

"Sit tight. I'm gonna reconnoiter the area. Find out where our lines are. Find out who's winning. You know small shit like that." Jim smiled, as if there was any doubt. That last remark brought some life back in Doug's face.

"Well, okay. I'm not going anywhere," he replied.

Once outside, Jim headed for the back gate at Fort Kobbe. It was warming up now, and he started to sweat. Just past the boulevard and where the beach bodegas started, he saw some army vehicles. As he got closer, he noticed soldiers. They had put concertina wire across the road. Off to one side was a Hummer with .30 calibers on top. As Jim got to within one hundred meters from the wire, a soldier hollered.

"Alto! Donde vas?"

"Poner sus manos arriba y vien aqui!"

Jim raised his hands and approached. "Yo, dude! I'm an American. I work at Howard, and I need to talk to whoever's in charge," Jim addressed the soldier.

"Captain!" he yelled back. "Got a civilian here, sir. Wants to talk to you, sir."

The officer reached in his pocket and pulled out a piece of paper. He unfolded it and looked at Jim.

"Name?" he asked.

"Hoeber. James W. Hoeber." Jim handed him his passport and military ID card.

The captain ran his finger down the list of names on the paper. "Name's not here. Where did you say you live?"

"Other side of town. Down past the hospital," Jim answered.

"You coming in?" the officer asked.

"No. No, I've got to get back to my wife and kids. I just need to know what the situation is, that's all." Jim didn't want to cross onto the base which was US property. Once he did, he would fall under the authority of the officer in charge and might not able to get back out. The captain called over to one of his troops. Jim now noticed the mortar emplacements on both sides of the road. One of the soldiers came over to the Hummer and spoke with the officer. They unfolded a map on the hood and called Jim to come over.

"Don't worry, we'll let you back out. Just show my guys here exactly where you live. If you know about any other Americans holed up in town, we need to know where they are at also," he said while pointing to the map.

Jim showed him what he wanted and got as much information as he could about the current situation. He then headed back to Doug's place. Doug was still on the phone. Jim waited.

"Okay, what's the—?" Doug stopped. A whop, whop, whop sound of a helicopter passed over the house.

Doug bent over and looked out the door. Jim told Doug, "Here's the situation. You've got a company of soldiers just down the road towards the base. They're set up with light and medium weapons. No armor, just infantry. I showed them on the map where we live so they shouldn't be dropping anything in on us." Jim gave him as much information as he had.

While Jim was gone, Doug had asked Evergreen to contact Jim's father in Texas to let him know that he and the family were okay. They talked for a few minutes more. Jim was in a hurry to get back home, so he took off.

Walking back through town, nothing had changed. No one said a word to him. It was like he was invisible. He walked all the way through town to the other side. As he crossed the small school bridge, he saw some commotion down at the hospital. There was a flat bed truck parked in front of the main doors. Several US soldiers were directing some of locals. There were about five to six army guys and about a dozen Panamanians. Now he could see what they were doing. They were offloading bodies and taking them into the hospital. These must have been the casualties from the last night. Jim stood there for a while. He thought he would go over and get a better look. Maybe he would see someone he knew. There were still about ten to fifteen bodies on the truck. It was hard to tell because of the way they were stacked, and some were messed up pretty good. He noticed that some had uniforms on which said that they were Panamanian Defense Force. The others wore regular street clothes. Some were missing parts. Others just looked dead. Jim asked one of the army troops where those guys came from. He said that they were from the garrison in town. The ones in "civies" had been found inside. Some were picked up off the street, and a few had met their end by acting "hostile."

Jim thought to himself, *Should have brought a camera.*

After a few minutes, he left and headed at a fast walk to the house. By now it was noon, and it was really getting warm. He had covered about six miles so far. He needed some water. As he got closer to the house, he debated with himself whether or not to tell Rosa about the bodies on the truck. He thought it better not to say anything just yet.

He had a lot to think about right then. Mainly, what's next. He still didn't know what was going on in town over the bridge. And especially what happened to the guys at the Caracol Hotel. How come nobody told him this shit was going down? He figured it was just SNAFU. Christmas this year was going to suck big time, he thought. Once back at his place, he felt better. Jim and Rosa talked. They spent the rest of the afternoon getting ready for when it gets dark. The radio station came back on that evening, and they listened to Radio Panama Canal. The TV was still off.

10 U.S. hostages escape captors

By RICHARD SISK
Daily News Staff Writer

PANAMA CITY — Ten Americans — kidnaped, tortured and threatened with sexual abuse and death by their Panamanian abductors — were rescued yesterday by a U.S. helicopter after escaping and hiding two nights on a jungle hillside.

The hostages, all employes of Evergreen International, a U.S. military aviation contractor, said they were constantly told by their captors, "You'll never see Christmas."

One of the captives, Don Davis, Evergreen's director in Panama, said the group's ordeal began early Wednesday during the first hours of the U.S. invasion.

Panamanian soldiers and members of dictator Manuel Noriega's so-called Dignity Battalions shot off the locks and bashed down the doors of the Panama City apartment building where the Americans were sleeping.

Naked, blindfolded

The Americans, some clad only in undershorts and others naked, were blindfolded and herded into a bus, Davis said.

Their captors drove them to an unknown location where the Americans were punched, stomped and beaten with rifle butts, Davis said. Several of the ex-hostages yesterday had badly bruised faces to testify to their mistreatment.

On Thursday, the Americans were moved to another location, placed in a room reeking of urine and feces, and beaten again, Davis said.

Nick Stollman, 28, said his tormentors favored "boot-kicking."

"They said we would never see Christmas, that we all deserved to die," Stollman said last night, shortly before boarding a U.S military flight for the United States. "It's hard to believe we're here now."

Stollman said his captors twice threatened him with sodomy, but instead chose to stomp on his bare back and try to break his ankles.

Later Thursday the group was moved to a school. There, the Americans resolved to escape. Several managed to slip out of the rope and wire that bound their hands behind their backs and to free their comrades. Davis speculated that nearly two days without food or water had helped him slip his hands out of their bonds.

When the group, made up of pilots, cargo handlers and other aviation workers, crept out a back door, they discovered their guards were nowhere in sight, Davis said.

The Americans hustled along a drainage ditch to one of the many hillside thickets that pock the Panama City landscape. Some of the men were still naked or clad only in underwear.

Finally, at noon yesterday, a U.S. helicopter spotted them, plucked them from the hillside and took them to Howard Air Force Base.

Seven of the hostages returned to the U.S. last night. Three others remain hospitalized — two for dehydration and one with a minor gunshot wound in the hand sustained when a guard fired into the ceiling to terrorize the hostages.

CHAPTER 13

Captured

The day had started quite suddenly in those early morning hours, December 20, 1989. Doug, Jim, and their families had fared pretty well. They were safe, and although things had been happening pretty fast, in all, it wasn't too bad. The Evergreen guys down at the Caracol didn't do as well, though. Their horrible experience wasn't learned until they showed up on Christmas eve.

That night, on the evening of the nineteenth, while Doug and Jim were moving the aircraft out a Howard AFB. Don Davis had just arrived back at the Caracol. Once he arrived, he sent two of the pilots, Tom Eastman and Nick Stolman, out to Torrijos Airport in the rental van to pick up an incoming pilot. He was due to arrive at 8:55 p.m. from the States. They picked him up and got back to the hotel around 11:00 p.m. After Bill McQuade, the new pilot, and Davis had talked for a while, Don gave him some company bedding. Bill got room number 57. It was next to Don Davis's room. Since it was getting late, they both turned in. The night was short lived, though.

At approximately 1:00 a.m., Wednesday, the twentieth of December, all hell broke loose. A loud explosion shook the hotel. Numerous large explosions went off in the old section of the city, Chorrillo. There were more blasts coming from Paitilla Airport, which was less than a mile away. There was automatic gunfire everywhere. It reverberated off the buildings. Panic was setting in. Those who were sound asleep one minute were suddenly awakened to the fact of war. This tropical paradise had instantly turned real nasty.

Davis got a phone call from the front desk. It was Mayea. Mayea worked nights and knew everyone. She was crying and very upset. She told Davis that the United States had just attacked Panama. She said it was on the TV. Davis turned it on, but just like everywhere else, the station was briefly on declaring a state of emergency, imminent hostile action expected, and all US personnel to take shelter immediately. "Do not go on the street. The US Military is presently engaged in combat with hostile Panamanian Defense Force throughout the republic." Then the TV went off the air also.

Sporadic gunfire continued on the streets below. Bullets could be heard ricocheting of cement walls. The horizon was ablaze. There were tracer rounds in red and white arcing across and over the city. Within a few minutes, Davis had dressed and went out on the balcony. Looking down, he saw armed Panamanian troops and Dignity Battalion personnel in the streets. There was no traffic, only people, armed people on foot. Suddenly the TV came back on.

"This is the Armed Forces Emergency Broadcast Station. PML ECHO is in effect. Do not go outside! Stay indoors! Lock all doors and windows! Do not, repeat, do not open the door for anyone!" Then it went back off.

For the next hour or so, the Evergreen guys watched what was going on in the streets below. At approximately 3:00 a.m., Mayea called from the front desk. She told Davis that there were PDF Forces at and now in the Caracol complex. Davis, stunned, thanked her and asked her to please let him know if hostilities increased to a point where they might have to evacuate. Peter Dickson called Don and wanted to know what was going on. Don was just getting ready to tell him that it might be a good idea to get the hell out of there when the phone went dead. Since this was an interhotel call, room to room, Davis suspected the lines up from the lobby had been cut. Don looked outside and didn't see anything. It was quiet outside, no close gunfire. Don tried the phone again, but it was still dead. He thought he might go down stairs but decided not to. After all, so far, so good. The others started to relax a little in the lull of things, also. Big mistake. While they should have been implementing a contingency plan in preparation for the worst, they instead became complacent. Complacency will get you dead real fast. They figured that the conflict was between the US Army and PDF, by now really pissed, thought otherwise.

Around 5:00 a.m., Don Davis received a phone call from the front desk. *How strange*, he thought, *the phone's back on.*

It was Mayea again. This time, she spoke loud and fast. She told him that there were heavily armed Panamanian Defense Troops at the door. They were breaking the glass and entering the hotel complex. She then screamed. Automatic rifle fire ensued. Davis could hear shouting and yelling over the phone.

"Mayea! Mayea! You okay? What's happening?" Davis shouted in the phone.

Nothing on the other end. Only silence. Don stood there, shocked. Suddenly a large explosion rocked the hotel. Plaster and dust fell from the ceiling. Now more automatic rifle fire. This time, it was close, real close. Davis moved to the door and leaning against it, tried to listen. He strained to hear something. Out in the hallway, there was a lot of yelling and screaming in Spanish. People were running past the door. There was a loud banging noise that sounded like someone kicking in doors. Davis had turned out the lights. It was dark, but he could still see somewhat. He was standing there when his door started to rattle. They were checking it to see if it was locked. They found it was and started to kick it in. Davis, still confident that the PDF would not harm any civilians, especially Americans, went to the door to open it. Just as he got to it and started to open the door, a burst of automatic weapon fire riddled the wall and door frame. The doorknob was blown completely off. With a loud boom, the door flew open, and armed PDF bolted in, rifles blazing. Luckily, Davis wasn't hit. However, one of the Panamanian ran up to Don and without saying a word, hit him square between the eyes with a rifle butt. Down he went. When he came to on the floor, there was a lot of blood around. He looked out the door, or what was left of it. There was a lot of people out in the hallway. There were Panamanians dressed in blue jeans and tennis shoes. Others had grenades. There was a great amount of commotion going on.

Bill McQuade, the new guy, was out in the hall. The armed men were beating him real bad. There was blood dripping off his fingers. There was wood sticking out of his arm. His clothes were ripped. Bill had been in his room holding the door closed when they shot through it. He had taken a round in the hand, and when the door splintered, he was in a bad way.

The PDF struck Davis several more times with rifle butts. One of them asked for his passport. Davis struggled to get up. He reached for his briefcase at the foot of the bed but was forced back on the floor with a gun barrel in his face. Finally, they dragged him out into the hallway where Bill McQuade was. Bill wasn't doing so good. He had just gotten in country at 9:00 p.m. that night. Now, less than eight hours later, this was happening. One of the PDF men came up to them, kicked Davis in the ribs, and yelled something in Spanish. Neither Bill nor Davis spoke Spanish. They had no idea what they wanted. One of the men pointed an AK-47 at Davis's head and yelled again.

Still they couldn't answer them, even being threatened with a shot in the head could not make them speak Spanish. Someone inside the room yelled, "Jefe." The PDF soldier who seemed to be in charge backed off and entered Davis's room. He thought that they probably had found whatever it was that they were looking for. They ransacked each room. After about twenty or thirty minutes of continual threats and beatings, Bill and Don were taken downstairs to the lobby. The others were already there.

Glancing around, Davis saw Don Campana, Vince Cardwell, and Jim Miller. Farther on in the lobby, the others were being held facedown on the floor. There was Joe Smith, Tom Eastman, Bill Farnan, Peter Dickson, and Nick Stolman. Miller and McQuade were sorta in the same boat. McQuade had just arrived in country, and Miller had been leaving country. He would have been long gone but for a lack of time, had decided to stay one more day, a decision he would regret for a long time. The Panamanians bound each person hands behind their back with rope and torn T-shirt strips. For the next hour or so, they were randomly kicked, beaten, and had rifle butts slammed into the back or their heads. The thugs threatened them with death for invading Panama. They were told for this they were worse than Cubans or Colombian drug dealers. That for invading their republic, they were guilty of the highest crime to humanity and that they would be shot at dawn.

The Panamanians began looking for the keys to the yellow rental van. They asked, in broken English, where they had hid the keys. No one said anything. Davis began to speak. He raised up a bit and told them that the van was a company rental from Budget. Before he could finish, he was kicked in the right side of the head. He blacked out. He drifted in and out of consciousness for the next half hour. Davis couldn't speak. He was disoriented. He thought the keys were on the dining room table. Tom Eastman had put them there upon his return from the airport.

After an hour or so more, they took everyone upstairs to room 12. All this time, no one had seen Mayea. They feared the worst. She had warned the Americans and therefore had collaborated with the enemy. This was surely a death sentence. Upstairs, the PDF threw them inside the room. Now all the Evergreen personnel were close together, except for Terry and Karen Olsen and Jim Ritter. They had gone out earlier to town, and their location was unknown. They were under armed guard but were able to whisper among themselves. They looked each other over and assessed the situation. They realized that no one had been seriously hurt to this point. All of them had been beaten. Some were bleeding but not from wounds that were life threatening. Of course, this whole situation was life threatening.

For the next two hours, the Panamanians ransacked their rooms. They took everything of value. Outside they placed pillow slips full of their loot in the hall. Now it was bright outside, and it was warming up. They remembered what they were told. They would be shot at dawn. They hoped they had lied because it was definitely past dawn. All this time, the PDF would come in and out of the room. Whenever one of them came in, they would kick or beat one or more of them. They continued to ask questions but got no answers. There was a language barrier as well as a general desire not to say anything that would start something. There were eight to ten well-armed men in the room with them. They were totally ruthless but lacked organization. Intent on terror tactics, they continued to threatened their prisoners. At several times, they were told they would never leave alive.

Davis tried to tell them that their enemy was the army, not them just mere, lowly civilians that knew nothing.

At approximately 9:00 a.m., the Evergreen group was were forced downstairs to the parking area under the apartments. A small bus was there waiting. The armed PDF captors forced them into the bus. They made them lie between the seats on the floor or in the aisle. When one of them wouldn't fit because they were bound or large, they were struck with rife butts. The Panamanians jumped on them till they fit. The main individual who seemed to be in charge did most of the assaulting. Later this person would be a deciding factor in their decision to escape. He continually called them "sons of a bitch" and that they would never see their families again. He said that they would all die, die in the same manner as the innocent Panamanian civilians who had died during the attack. He told them they would be chopped into pieces, beheaded, and the parts thrown over the wall of the United States Embassy. They produced machetes and waved them around, poking their prisoners in the back and face.

The bus trip took thirty minutes or so. It was hard to tell how long as they had taken everyone's watches. Thirty minutes was a good estimate, though. After all, these guys were pilots and aircrew members and used to precise time increments. They were surely within a minute or two. Davis assumed that they were still in occupied Panamanian-controlled areas. He estimated they had gone fifteen miles, more or less, outside of Panama City. Most likely toward the international airport or toward Colon. Finally the bus came to a stop. They were at a compound of some sort in the foothills off a dirt road. It was surrounded by a tall cinder block and chain-link fence. The bus was backed in. Once it stopped, everyone was ordered off. As they exited the bus, they were struck with rifle butts or prodded with machetes, all the time being yelled at viciously. They were shoved into a building and thrown on the floor. The room was solid cement. The wall and floor were solid, no windows and only one door. It looked like a storage room of some sort, or maybe a vault.

For the next several hours, no attempt to communicate was made. Every so often, one of the captors would enter and pick one of the guys for beating. They all were lying on their stomachs with hands still bound tight behind their backs. Now they returned and bound their feet together. One of the Panamanians started beating them with a section of air hose with the air chuck still in it. They walked on their bodies, stomping on their backs and heads. They lifted them up by their bound arms, kicked, and stomped on elbows and knees. They were trying to inflict as much damage as possible. Another PDF assailant had a radiator hose with wire showing. He would thrash them, trying to hit the eyes. If one of them cried out, they would call him "Rambo" and assault him even more. Joe Smith, who was facedown on the floor, was covered with blood. The whole side of his face was bloody, and his hair was matted. Joe had been kicked in the side of the head opening, a large split over his right eyelid and down the side of the eye socket. He had been, and still was, bleeding profusely, but the captors weren't concerned in the slightest. He appeared unconscious. After some time, the men left and went outside. Davis didn't know if they had just gotten tired or were going to just take a break and return in short order. After a few minutes, one guy came back with a water hose and the water was scalding hot. At first they thought the PDF was trying to burn them, but the water soon turned cold. Davis realized that the water was hot at first because the hose had been lying outside in the sun. They seemed to take great pleasure in spraying their prisoners. Laughing, they tried to force the water down the throats of some of them. After the PDF thugs washed down the whole place and everyone was drenched, they left and chained the door. It was jet black inside, and now it was getting cold. Goose bumps came up on Davis. They all lay there shivering from shock, being beat, wet and scared. The only sounds were the moaning, gurgling sound Joe Smith was making from the corner.

After a few hours had passed, the captors came in, and everyone was forced to stand. They picked up Joe and were herded into a waiting covered two-and-a-half ton truck. They were forced in at gunpoint. Some were physically thrown in. The truck drove off down a bumpy road. After about thirty minutes, they stopped for a moment. Davis felt that they were being driven further out of the city toward the northeast. He wasn't for sure, though, as they couldn't see out. The canvas coverings were closed tight. It was stuffy and hot. There were also three armed guards in the back with them. The truck stopped several time en route to converse with people. Then they would continue on. It was not known what they were talking about, but Davis was sure it concerned the status of the road ahead. Finally the truck stopped at another compound. This one was on the side of a hill. It too was surrounded by a cinder block wall. After the truck entered, the prisoners were taken to the main building. This compound was more fortified than the previous one. It was probably a garrison of the PDF regulars. There were a lot more soldiers here. Most were heavily armed and seemed in a state of high anxiety. These troops had "kill" written all over them. Davis thought Bat 2000 or some sort of special forces. At any rate, he sure didn't want to be turned over to them. The prisoners were escorted through what appeared to be some sleeping quarters, then down a long hallway to some jail cells. The one they had stopped at had a Panamanian civilian inside already. The PDF took him out and let him go free. Davis and the others, all ten of them, were shoved inside and the cell door locked. The cell was approximately five feet by nine feet. Not much room, especially for ten. The floor was made of hard clay or cement. There were no windows. The entire front was iron bars of about two inches diameter. The whole cell reeked of urine and feces. Huge cockroaches darted everywhere. As they walked around, the floor made sticky noises, like when you spill Coke on the floor and don't wipe it up. There were stains on the walls that appeared to be old blood. The floor had similar stains. Any remaining clothing was removed from them. The ones that had underwear on were allowed to keep it on. Those who didn't have underwear on because of what had happened earlier and how they were initially captured were forced to stay nude. While they were taking their clothes, Davis asked for drinking water and medical attention for Joe. Joe was extremely weak from his ordeal. He was pale and spoke incoherently. Davis, for his concern, was answered with a gun barrel being showed in his face. One by one, each was ordered to the cell door where the clothes were collected. The guards cut up some of the clothes to make gags. These they applied as hard as they could make them. Dozens of people were paraded past the cell, poking them with machetes and pulling their hair. Some were in uniform, others wore civilian clothes.

All this time, they were being threatened with death at any moment. After an hour or so, a PDF officer appeared. He clearly was in charge, and the other soldiers snapped to attention when he passed. He wore the rank of a major. He approached and started asking questions. Since this was a person who commanded authority and since he spoke in Spanish, Bill Farnan, one of the plane captains, came forward and admitted that he knew a little Spanish and could translate. Up till now, he had been silent, thinking that if the PDF didn't know he spoke Spanish, they would talk normally. That way, they would know what was going to happen before it happened. Farnan gave him their names and translated their job descriptions. He told him that they worked for Evergreen, which was a civilian company and nonhostile. Farnan explained that it was their job fly throughout Central America providing logistical support for the US government as well as other foreign governments, countries that included Panama upon request. He added that Evergreen had Panamanian government approval to work in Panama, and even Noriega himself had Casa 212s at Patilla.

"If you would just check," he said, "our contract is on public record at the Assembly."

This was a lie, but considering the situation, public records and or checking with the government was probably not possible. Once again, the PDF asked about the keys to the yellow van. What the big deal was about concerning the van was anybody's guess. Farnan told the officer that the first group of captors had taken the keys at the Caracol. They had said they would Davis told him to be calm and everything would be all right. Vince was concerned that he might die. Davis reassured him that he was not. Shortly the Panamanian officer returned to the cell and told them that the man who had fired into the cell area was drunk and would be punished. This was not good news. Not only were these guys hostile, now they were drunk too! Davis asked the officer for medical attention for Joe, Vince, and

Bill. He looked at them and left. During the next couple of hours, they were left alone. However, they were closely watched. When no one was watching, Davis loosened the blinding on Vince's hands. He had said that he was losing the feeling in his fingers. Davis swapped places an got them room to lay down.

Joe's right forehead was completely swollen. He couldn't see and was blind in the right eye. The whole side of his face had turned blue. His eye was completely closed. He still oozed blood from the wound, and blood had run down his body and right arm. Everyone in the cell had blood on them. They whispered to each other, asking who got hit and who didn't. It was now getting dark, and there was a commotion on the floor. There was also a lot of activity in the compound area. It sounded like they were getting ready for an attack that might come after dark. That afternoon, there had been sporadic small arms fire within a mile of there. Several loud explosions had also been heard in the same direction.

Just after dusk, a nurse arrived. She asked to see Joe and Vince. She spoke English and after speaking briefly with Joe, she said she would return later. Another lie but maybe it would buy them some time, or at least cast doubt on who wanted what. The officer left to check out Bill's story. For Bill's help in translating, he was bound with a large rope across his mouth. This was pulled as tight as possible, securing his head against the iron bars of the cell door. He was then poked repeatedly with knifes. The cell being extremely small, the others that were up against the bars were poked as well. Intimidating the prisoners, the guards would draw a knife across their throats, indicating that they were going to slit their throats. Bill hung on the bars for hours. He was visibly weakening. He was, after all, in his late fifties. While he was hanging there, a PDF regular walked up and opened fire into the cell with his AK-47. Bullets, brass, and cement chips flew throughout the cell. Vince Cardwell was struck in the head and dropped to floor, bleeding profusely. Everyone was piled up on the floor except for Bill, who was still hanging there. The guard reloaded and emptied another chip into the cell. They lay on the floor motionless, scared shitless, not daring to move a muscle. After waiting for what seemed like hours, Davis looked up. The guard was gone. Davis started to loosen the rope on his hands and finally managed to free himself. He checked Vince for a pulse and general condition. Vince had received a glancing shot to the head. There was a long open wound across his scalp. The bullet had cut down to the bone but didn't penetrate the skull. The bleeding had slowed, and Vince wasn't going to die. He was in shock, though. Vince was shaking violently.

The nurse came back and gave him a large shot in the buttocks. It was probably penicillin or some other powerful antibiotic. She gave him another smaller one in the arm. Joe staggered and almost fell to the floor. He was visibly weak from the ordeal. Joe got the same shots. Bill Farnan was okay. Bill McQuade was looked at but didn't receive any shots as the nurse determined that the wound to his hand wasn't that bad. After the nurse left, the guards left and cut Farnan down. Everyone was ordered to stand. Those that were naked were given pants. These pants were the same as ones taken from them earlier that day. After they dressed, they were removed from the cell and marched single file down the hall. A guard checked each person's binding as they passed. This really pissed the PDF off. After a big stink about it, they put regular handcuffs on them. Joe received a set as well. Once outside, the PDF forced them into a waiting ambulance. The blindfolds were put back on as they entered the vehicle. It wasn't totally dark yet, but the sun had been down a long time.

Jim Miller and Peter Dickson sat across from Davis. Joe Smith was lain across Jim and Peter's lap. Two armed PDF guards and the nurse accompanied the driver up front. Jim Miller lay on the floor. Vince Cardwell sat to the right of Davis. Next to Vince was another armed PDF guard. The other five, Donny Campana, Tom Eastman, Nick Stolman, Bill McQuade, and Bill Farnan, were loaded into another truck with more armed PDF guards and brought up the rear. The convoy of truck, ambulance, and escort vehicles pulled out the compound and drove for about thirty minutes or so. Most of the trip was along hard surface roads. They didn't speed but maintained about thirty miles per hour. Jim Miller, who was on the floor, started complaining that the floor was getting real hot. The PDF guards paid no attention. They just looked and laughed. Davis and Vince slid their feet under him to raise him up a little of the floor. It didn't help much, but a little bit was better than nothing at all.

After a while, they arrived at a large three-story school building. Once out of the vehicles, they were taken to a small open room. By that time, it was totally dark outside. Davis had managed to get his blindfold off. He now worked on his handcuffs. For some reason, the latch on his right cuff wasn't good and after twisting it back and forth, managed to get it open. Now he had his hands free. One by one, the PDF guards would come in and take a prisoner out of the room. At that time, no one knew what was happening to them or where each was taken. When all the prisoners had been removed, they learned that they each had been checked individually. Now they were all together again under a stairwell. Only one armed guard was watching them. The beatings had stopped. These new PDF guards seemed to be a little more friendly. Davis and a few of the others thought about jumping the guard. They decided not to. The risk was to great, with four of the ten injured. After a half hour under the stairs, they were taken to a classroom. Again they were all together again. They felt better. Relief came as their new cell was a little more comfortable than the previous places of incarceration. The classroom had two tables a couch, two padded chairs, and several plastic chairs. On one side of the room were large draped windows that you could not see through. The wall where the windows were also had two metal doors. Between the doors were about twenty feet of small locked individual school lockers. They were told to sit down and be quiet.

Shortly, a man in a white guayabera shirt and slacks came in and addressed the prisoners. He spoke in Spanish and in broken English with authority. This guy was definitely important. The PDF officer stood at attention when they came in. None of the guys knew him. However, Davis assumed he was an intelligence officer. Bill Farnan translated when he spoke in Spanish. The man said he was "Manos Negro," black hand, as they were known to come at night and people disappeared, Never to be seen again. Or maybe secret police. At any rate, he looked serious.

"You people are prisoners of war and are being held as much. You are considered by the Panamanian Provisional Government to be spies or operatives of the Central Intelligence Agency. Our country has been attacked by the United States and is presently engaging your soldiers in heavy combat on several fronts and several provinces in the interior," he said sternly. He told them that they were hostages. They would be held for a minimum of twenty-four hours more. Escape was impossible.

"If you try to escape, or we even think you are trying to escape, you will be shot immediately on sight. This is not a joke or a game."

He added that a deal with US Forces, SOUTHCOM was in process and if they wanted to live, to do exactly as they were told. Suddenly the power generator stopped. The lights went out, and it was pitch black. The three PDF persons that were in the room speaking left and locked the door. Davis and the others could hear the guards talking coming from outside windows. They stayed quiet, straining to hear anything. Some of the captives mentioned that they were hungry. They had not had any food for twenty-four hours, no water since that morning. Davis took off his gag and undid the partially secured handcuff. He then went from person to person, losing their bindings. Everyone was freed except for Vince and Joe, who wore handcuffs. It was extremely dark inside the room. Without some light and some sort of tools or lockpicks, getting the handcuffs off was almost impossible right then. They all found a place to stretch out. Although it got pretty cold that night, maybe in the low fifties, most were able to nap in spite of all the pain that had been inflicted that day. Vince and Joe were in the most pain because of the wounds. They still were cuffed, which makes it difficult to get comfortable, much less get some sleep. As often as possible, someone would rub their shoulders to keep circulation going and warm them up. The rest of the night, they tried to get some sleep, but most just lay there and moaned. It wasn't a good day. Almost half the group had been wounded or injured. All had been tortured and beat severely.

C H A P T E R   1 4

Escape and Freedom

Jim awoke to the sounds of a helicopter hovering in the street directly in the front gate. Operation Just Cause had been going on now for a little over twenty-four hours. This day, December 21, was already starting out weird. He had slept with his clothes on, just in case he had to jump up and hightail it out of there at a moment's notice. It didn't take him long to get out to where the Black Hawk was setting down. He opened the iron gate and stepped out.

The helo had already landed on the road. An air crewman was standing beside it with a flight helmet on and a ground cord attached to the bird. Jim crossed over the street and approached the helicopter. Out of nowhere, a soldier with an M-16 popped up and ordered him to stop in no uncertain terms. Just as this was happening, another army soldier came running up with two small children in his arms. This followed by a Panamanian girl and her army husband. It was now apparent that this was an evac craft sent in the retrieve a US soldier's family. They loaded up in a flash. The crewman on the headset hollered to Jim loudly.

"You American? If so, get your ass on board. We're out of here. If you don't want out, then you're on your own. Last chance."

Jim was just standing there as he grabbed his cord and dove in. The Black Hawk powered up and away.

"'Last chance'? What's that supposed to mean?" Jim stood there, looking up and mumbling, "Last chance! Oh shit! I don't like the sound of that."

Jim sprinted back to the house. Just as he got back to the iron gate, he noticed someone had piled up a bunch of cement blocks at the corner of the front wall. He knew what that was. Someone was planning on jumping over the wall and had made themselves a staircase. He picked up the blocks, tossing them over the eight-foot-high wall. He remembered that first night and the face that he saw looking over a wall in that exact spot. If they wanted in, they were just going to have to get some more blocks. The electricity was back on. Jim checked all the outside lights. He wanted plenty of light outside and on the wall perimeter come nightfall. Going to work was definitely out of the question, so he resolved himself to the idea that if they wanted him, they knew where to find him. "They," as far as work goes, being only Doug. Everyone else was still unaccounted for.

Nothing much happened that day until midafternoon. Suddenly gunfire started up again. It was close but not that close. The neighbors had told Rosa that there was sniper fire in town. Bullets had been coming in off the mountain for the last several hours. The army had been returning with mortar fire. Jim figured he would stay inside for the time being. At about four o'clock, Jim heard a bunch of noise outside in the front. He looked out the window and could see some American soldiers that had parked a Humvee in front of his front wall next to the front gate. They were real busy doing something, so he thought he'd go check it out. He opened up the gate and poked his head out. Jim couldn't believe what he saw. There were a bunch of army guys unloading sandbags and stacking them up to make a bunker. One of the soldiers, not doing any work, came over and spoke to Jim. He was drawn by the look of disbelief on Jim face.

"Hey, man. You the American dude that lives here?" he asked.

"Yeah," Jim answered.

"Well, we're going to keep you company for a while."

"Like hell you are. If you guys want to build a fort someplace and draw fire all night, then why don't you go down the road someplace and camp! Next thing you'll be wanting to do is fly and American flag off a palm tree or something. Hey, I know. Go get me some white paint and I'll paint a big bull's-eye on my roof." Jim was pissed off. The soldiers left.

For the Evergreen captives, the twenty-first had been a little better. They were no longer being beaten and tortured. Isolated, they had more time to themselves. By now several of the guys had to go to the bathroom. There wasn't one in the classroom, so they looked around for something that would suffice. They found a large potted plant in the corner that would serve as a urine depository for the ten of them. Somehow they saw humor in peeing in the pot. When school resumes sometime later on and the day got hot, you could imagine what would be going on. Around nine o'clock, it had warmed up. One of the guards was at door, unlocking it. Everyone scrambled to their places and resumed their "hands behind your back" positions. One of the guards brought in water. They all drank. Bill Farnan asked if Joe and Vince might have their handcuffs loosened. The guards agreed, reluctantly, but refused to reposition them in front.

They said they didn't have authorization to do that. One of guards attempted to adjust Davis's as well. Davis told them his were fine. Davis could take his off and on at will because they were broken. He didn't want them to discover this. The guards stayed in the room with them for a while and then left. Around midday, the voice of an additional guard was heard. It was the voice of one of the original captors, specifically the most brutal one. The voice of the one that shot Vince and kicked Joe's head in. They knew they were not safe as long as this individual and possibly his group knew they were there. They did not want to be put into a situation where this guy could shoot all of them or lob a hand grenade into the classroom. They were afraid that now the beatings would resume. It was at that moment, upon hearing his voice, that they made up their minds collectively about escaping if the opportunity presented itself. They were driven by fear and if required, kill.

All afternoon, they searched the room for items that may be useful to them later. They found some wire from the back of a picture hanging on the wall. With this, they picked the locks on the school lockers. They found a backpack, a cardboard cutting knife, crate paper in various colors, material, and cloth items that could be used as foot wrappings. One of the lockers produced a mirror, a hairbrush, some pencils, and a wooden ruler. They put all the items in the backpack and stowed it in an unlocked locker. They worked as quietly as possible, not knowing when the guards would return. They discussed the escape. They talked about breaking out the windows, but there were bars on them. They checked to see if they could bust through the wall. This would get them into the adjoining classroom. Davis wanted to remove the decorative square cement ventilation blocks at the ceiling. Then sliding outside. They checked the second door at the rear of the room. Up till now, this door hadn't been used at all. They discovered that apparently it was locked from the class-room side and could be opened. If there wasn't a hasp and lock on the hall side, then it could be used for the escape exit. Very quietly Davis pulled the door open. He hoped it didn't squeak. It didn't. He opened it about an inch. Peering out, he discovered that there was nothing locking the door from the hall side. Davis smiled at the others. Excellent, they found a way out, at least out to the hall. They spent the rest of the afternoon preparing for the escape. They had all agreed that their situation was ominous, and they did not want to die. That would really suck. They had been injured, tor-tured, shot, beaten, threatened, intimidated, and taken to the edge. Now they made the decision not to be bargaining material and, if possible, deny their captors any possible gain they might enjoy by continuing to hold them prisoner. However, the escape would carry an element of danger. It was agreed that if anyone had any doubts about the planned escaped, it was necessary to discuss it right then. They all agreed to go.

The plan was to call out to the guards for water. This would locate their position outside the room. If they got no response, they would call out again. If they still got no response, they would exit the door. If caught in the act, they would claim they were looking for water, not escaping. If successful and undetected, they planned to exit the school by any door.

Once outside and clear of the building, they were to head east away from the gunfire in the west. The shooting had been severe the night before. Once out and clear of the building, they would scatter and go to a hilltop that they had seen from the rear window of the classroom. They would wait there until every one was accounted for. If all were safe and had not been seen, they planned on staying there as long as possible. If in two days they had not been rescued, they would leave. They would try to signal aircraft that flew over with the mirror. If it got too dangerous to remain there, they would proceed to a large house that could be seen on one of the hilltops nearby. From there, they would try to phone or signal again. If possible, try to acquire a vehicle and drive out to find some friendly forces. There was also a telephone outside the classroom in the hall. The guards had been trying to use it previously that night. Sometimes they had gotten it to work, sometimes not. The Evergreen prisoners realized that they wouldn't be able to use it as it was a pay phone and they had no money. Just before sunset, they fabricated footwear from the material taken out of the lockers. Davis and Nick Stolman had managed to pick the locks on the handcuffs Joe and Vince were wearing. They did this with curtain hooks from the drapes. They kept the handcuffs just in case they might have to take prisoners themselves or maybe leave somebody secured to a pipe or something. Davis removed two of the drapery panels and repositioned the remaining drapes so as to cover the missing parts. The drapes were about eight foot by five foot in size. These drapes could be used for many things. Blankets, stretcher, shelter covers were some of their possible uses. They cleaned the room as carefully as possible, putting everything back in its original position. They planned to exit and pull the chairs back against the door. They hoped that anyone entering through the other door would think that they had been removed by some of the other PDF guards. They hoped no one would realize they had escaped until they were long gone. The time, the method, the manner, and a contingency plan was set. They were ready.

About fifteen minutes past sunset, they began calling for water. There was no answer. They called out again. There was no answer. The door opened slowly. Davis looked down the hall. He didn't see anyone. He then made his way down the hall and looked out into the school yard. No one was there either. He noticed that there were some military vehicles parked on the side. He went back down the hall and found the restroom. Staying in the shadows, he scouted the immediate area. There was water in the rest room. Back at the classroom, Davis briefed the others as to where the water was. It was in the plan to drink as much water as possible before going into the jungle. This they would do as long as there was no sign of the PDF. Davis went out first. He checked the back side of the school building. The slope down the hillside looked clear. This was the planned escape route. When he got back inside, the others told him that the water was off. They checked the toilet tanks.

They were empty. They would have to get water some other way. Ready to go, the group assembled at the rear of school building. There was a large open area they had to cross before heading down the hill. They were pumped up. It was now or never.

"Okay, listen!" Davis said. "Everybody knows what to do. For the guys new to the program, it's not always like this. We'll cross in the group of three. Everybody meets in the darkness at the bottom of the hill. Recognition password will be 'Casper 212.' Casper 212 was the call sign for the CASA 212 Program. Sprinting across the open area as fast as they could, the three-man groups dove into the jungle. They all made it and apparently had not been detected. This was a great relief. They had expected gunshots as any moment. Within ten minutes of leaving the classroom, they were at the bottom of the hill and partly in the jungle. It was extremely dark, swampy, infested with mosquitoes, and filled with black palms. Black palm are the type of palm tree that has thousands of needle-sharp thorns up to three inches in length, running the full length of the trunk.

These needle-like spines are mildly poisonous and are brittle. This makes them hard to remove from the skin. They can puncture leather gloves. Several other types of palms also posses these type of thorns and are plentiful in the tropics. Fifty yards or so into the jungle, they encountered a barbwire fence. As they crossed the fence, Bill Farnan went down the fence line and was separated from the group. When they discovered him missing, they called out softly but got no answer. It was too dark to search for him, so they decided to wait for five minutes. If he didn't show, they would move on the hilltop, putting as much distance between them and the schoolhouse as possible. This was paramount. They could not afford to be recaptured. The

PDF had made it very clear that if they attempted to escape, they would be executed. The group moved on easterly and deep into the jungle. They did not know what would happed next in this snake-infested swamp, but they did know that they were free from the PDF and weren't going back. The jungle got thicker, and the going got slower. It was difficult. There were many overhanging branches laced with vines. The ground was a sucking muck filled with leeches and stumps. It was so dark that they couldn't see their hands in front of their face. They trudged on blindly. They proceeded on by feel only. Coming across a ravine, they stayed in the bottom and followed the stream. After about an hour, they stopped, listened for anything unusual. They got out the cup they had brought from the lockers. Straddling the stream, they took turns dipping water. They drank till full. There were no sounds other than the normal jungle noise. Up till now, it seemed, no one had discovered they were gone. At least they hoped so. After a short rest, they continued on along the streambed. Sometimes they moved along on hands and knees. Everyone stayed in single file, keeping close to the person in front by touch. Crossing several waterfalls made the going even slower. The curtains came in handy now. They used them to lower each other down the drop-offs. After about a mile, they came to a cliff. Tom Eastman tossed some rocks over the side. It sounded like quite a ways to the bottom. The water ran over the edge and turned into mist. They couldn't be for sure, but it sounded like it did. This was a good place to stop. There was the cliff to their backs and steep side up from the stream. They didn't want to traverse the drop off in the dark. If someone fell and was seriously injured. they would be in big trouble. It was pitch black dark, the area unfamiliar, and they needed to get bearings before going on. Joe Smith went up the bank on the right to find a flat spot. Tom Eastman checked the area on the left. Pete Dickinson went back down the stream to watch the rear for anyone who might be trailing them. After Joe and the others returned, they went up on the bank on the right to a flat spot in the grass. They spread out the drapes and rested on them. They were totally soaked. Along with the injuries they had received from the PDF, they were now covered with cuts from the saw grass and wounds from stinging nettle. The jungle, contrary to what some might think, is hostile to those who don't live in it. The spot they chose wasn't that flat but would suffice. They stomped out an area in the fifteen-foot-high elephant grass. They put one curtain drape on the ground and covered with the other. This was the best they could do. Luckily the bugs were not bad. It was cold and damp. Everyone was pretty much exhausted from their ordeal. Even so, they still didn't get much rest. The group was still pumped up from the escape and had no regrets about what they had done. They were at least free, free at last. It shouldn't be long before they were rescued, they hoped. The Evergreen group was intact and all together except for Bill Farnan. Bill's location was of much concern. It was obvious all were not comfortable with the idea that one of them was unaccounted for. They wondered what had happened to him. They also wondered how Jim and Doug had fared during the initial attack.

CHAPTER 15

Camp Quarry

Friday, December 22, started around 4:30 a.m. for the Evergreen group in the grass. They awoke to the sound of a flight of five CH-47 helicopters passing directly over their position at low level. Standing up, they could hear C-130 gunships working to the west of them and in the same general area of the schoolhouse that they had been held at the night before. Maybe the PDF in the area were preoccupied.

Toward first light, Peter Dickinson shook Davis. He had heard voices. It sounded like Bill Farnan talking to someone in Spanish. It came the direction of the schoolhouse and about a hundred yards or so from their position. In the early morning stillness and with the absence of night noise, he could just barely be heard. After about ten minutes, it got quiet, and there were no longer any sounds coming from that direction. There was some discussion about trying to find Bill. However, the terrain and circumstances didn't warrant splitting up the group. Shortly after sunrise, it started to get warm in the grass. The group moved back down to the stream. They drank more water and made preparations to put more distance between them and the schoolhouse. For sure, their escape had been discovered by now. If they were being tracked, they need to get moving. The group was unfamiliar with jungle navigation. This was Panama and the Panamanians' turf. The water was formidable. It was a good thing they didn't try to go down it at night. It was sheer drop of twenty feet to a flat solid rock bottom. The cliff was slick and offered no footing or handholds. They tied the curtain drapes together. Davis was lowered to the bottom. He secured the end. The others came down to the lower level with help from each other. The rest of the morning was spent following the streambed to the east. Some of the going was easy, but most of it was pretty tough. The space was set for the slowest member of the group. This was Jim Miller. He was dehydrated and was running a fever. They would travel for a hundred yards and stop to rest. After fifteen minutes, they would go again. Rounding a bend in the stream, they suddenly found footprints in the muddy side of the water. It looked like boots. Now they proceeded slower and more cautiously. Several times, they made side trips, trying to find some higher trail. They needed to get bearings again and try to signal if they saw an aircraft. No trails were found, so they continued along down the stream. This was a good choice because of the availability of water and the small aquatic animal life that could be eaten. One thing that bothered them was their inability to find edible vegetation. This problem was due to their lack of knowledge about jungle survival. The Panamanian jungle is a gold mine of edible plants. All palm fruit is edible, as well as over fifty different types of fruit-bearing trees and shrubs: banana, Nance, Marañon (cashew), mamon, guava. Also otoe, yame, yampre, berro, yucca, cassava, pan arbol. All grew along streambeds throughout Panama. Bill Farnan was knowledgeable about what plants to eat, but he was gone. There were other things to eat as well. The problem was that these men needed other things to eat as well. The problem was that these men were flight crew—pilots, not Green Beret jungle survival instructors. They observed that there were a lot of parasol ants. If it came right down to it, they would eat these. Although it hadn't been that long since the initial engagement, they realized that if they were going to stay out many more days, they would have to start collecting something to eat.

They continued on at the same pace. Later in the day, they found a dirt road that ran east and west. Peter and Nick Stolman crossed the road and hid in the grass on the other side. Don Campana crossed over and joined them. While the three of them waited and watched the deserted road, Tom Eastman and Don Davis paralleled the road to try to find some high ground. They wanted it to be in close proximity to the road and where they could signal any approaching friendly forces at the same be able to conceal themselves from the enemy, should they come along. Finally on the same side of the road as the main group, they found a rock quarry. It was about two hundred yards from where they crossed the road and about a hundred yards east of it. The quarry had been unused for many years. The jungle was in the process of reclaiming it. While Tom waited on the side of the road, Davis climbed up into the quarry and located a small area that could be used as a camp. It also afforded a location from which they could keep watch on the road. The open quarry provided a means to signal any aircraft that might fly over with out the enemy seeing them. Tom waited at the spot where the quarry was while Davis returned to get the others. Just as he got to the group, they noticed two Panamanians coming down the road. They were talking as if nothing was going on. Everyone had time to take cover, and they weren't seen. As they passed, it appeared they were unarmed, but Davis wasn't sure. He had to be sure, a hundred percent sure. They wore camouflage and looked hostile. Davis told the group to proceed down the road, in the grass one by one. They would find Tom Eastman, and he would direct them further on the quarry. The three on the other side of the road crossed over to where the others were. One by one, they left. Davis would count to ten and send another. Within an hour, everyone had made it, except for Jim Miller. Miller, being ill with fever, should not have been sent out on his own. He didn't show. Evidently he just kept on going and wandered off down the road, disoriented and dazed. This was not good. He could die before they could find him. He could be captured and compromise their location getting everyone killed. Davis looked around. Joe was gone.

"Damn it!" Davis exclaimed. "Everybody stay put. We need to be all together when we get rescued." Since Joe was the last one to see him, he figured he could find him, so he just took off. Blind in one eye and all. Joe didn't find him, but a small Panamanian boy of about seven came out of the brush and startled Joe. The boy gave Joe an orange and his Bible. Joe started freaking out. Here amid this horrible battle-torn, death-at-any-moment situation, this child was offering him food and his Bible.

"Man, they're not going to believe this," Joe said to himself.

The boy took off his white T-shirt and handed it to Joe. He was caked in blood and mud and surely looked like he needed it. Joe took the T-shirt, squinting at him through one eye. The boy smiled. Joe said, "Gracias."

The boy said, "Da nada," and disappeared back into the jungle. Joe stood there for a moment, bewildered. If he didn't have an orange, Bible, and T-shirt in his hands, he would have thought he had been hallucinating. Joe couldn't find Miller. He returned to the quarry and related his encounter with a local.

After about an hour, Pete and Don Campana left out to find Miller. Going in pairs was better that alone. They left out the quarry from the back side center. They were going to try to find first and then try and locate a small village that they had seen from the schoolhouse. Miller was not in good shape. They couldn't afford to keep losing people. Miller wasn't even supposed to be here. He should be in the States somewhere getting ready for Christmas. They had lost two people in two days. Everyone was on edge. Around five hours later, Pete and Don still hadn't made it back. Davis was getting real concerned as they were getting to spread out.

Then just before dusk, Peter and Don came in. They had Jim Miller with them. Miller was delirious. He was burning hot with fever. He didn't even know who he was or where he was. As they got Miller taken care of, Peter told them that they didn't find the village. Peter and Don, after leaving the quarry, had been following this road when they walked up on a group of Panamanians. They ducked into the bushes and listened. One of the men was pointing up the road and telling others something he saw. Whatever it was he saw, they were excited about it. One of the Panamanians was on the motorcycle and spotted Pete and Don as they exited the jungle a mere fifty feet from where they were talking on the road. They seemed as surprised as Pete and Don were. Pete and Done dove back into the jungle. The man on the motorcycle stopped, jumped off, and opened fire full auto into the bushes. Bullets zipped through the underbrush within inches of their heads. Another man joined in, and the automatic rifle fire increased. Pete and Don scrambled up the hill on their stomachs. After a few minutes, they stopped firing. Pete and Don stooped low and ran at a forty-five-degree angle to the road and intersected it around five hundred yards up from the spot where they first ran into the group of Panamanians. They crossed back over the road, and there, lying in the grass, was Jim Miller. He wasn't moving, so Pete checked for a pulse. Jim suddenly bolted up in sitting position. He was okay. Apparently he had lain down to rest and gone to sleep. Pete suspected it was more like passed out. They suspected he had heat exhaustion. His skin was white, cold, and clammy. They got him up. Because they were so close to the road, they had to move further into the bushes. There was also renewed hostile activity in the area. It would be unwise to stay in one spot for too long. From the time they picked up Miller to the time they made it back to the quarry was about an hour. They had stopped several times to cover their tracks. They had backtracked and left false marks. They wanted to make sure they weren't followed. Everyone was glad to see them back but not to happy to learn that there were still armed enemy in the immediate area.

By evening, they had located an easy access to the stream. It only took about fifteen minutes to go and bring back water. They used a plastic sack that they had found at the school. While Bill McQuade and Vince Cardwell were getting water, an army helicopter had flown over. They signaled or at least tried to with the mirror. They got no response. They had tried once earlier also. They assumed no one was looking for them, so it would be hard to get someone's attention. As time passed, it got darker. It was quiet at the quarry; however, there was a lot of small arms fire mixed with larger explosions around and down the hill. The guys made bed of leaves and cleared some spots to spend the night. They made one last trip to get water and bedded down just before it got totally dark. The mosquitoes were bad at the quarry. The attacked relentlessly until the night air temperature got down into the low fifties. Then the bugs weren't as active. The only true escape from the voracious insects was under the drape. Everyone couldn't fit under the drape at once, so they took turns. It was a lot warmer under the drape than outside. Once a person started shivering, he rotated in and the next guy out. The night passed with chattering of teeth and loud snoring. Occasionally soft talking was heard, and although they slept, it wasn't quality sleep. There were a lot of rocks, bits of machinery, and enough material to start fire, but they didn't want to give away their position. Since they knew nothing about what was going on and there was serious gunfire still going on within a quarter mile of the quarry, everyone thought it best not to start up fire. After all, this was Panama, not Alaska. You might be cold, but you sure as hell aren't going to freeze to death. Tomorrow's sunrise would bring warmth. After an hour in the sun, the cold of the night before would be only a memory.

Rescued

Sunrise was a welcome sight. It had been unusually cold last night. Once the sun was up, the quarry heated up fast as you would expect. They didn't think about it at the time, but the mere fact that this was a rock quarry would explain the extreme temperatures. The stone was cold at night and hot as hell in the afternoon. Today was Saturday, December 23. Tomorrow was Christmas Eve.

The morning brought some uneasiness among the group. Some of them were getting disillusioned by the fact that they had not made contact with any friendly forces. There was some talk about striking out toward town and making contact with whoever they might find, friendly or not. Peter and Davis kept reassuring them that help would come, just hold on. Just because they were tired, hungry and injured was no reason to give up. They had been through the worse escapes, and they would face death if captured. They figured that was about right and there was no justification to give in. After discussing all other options, they decided to stay for another twenty-four hours at the quarry in accordance with the original plan

With that settled, Davis and Vince went across to the other side of the quarry to an old iron generator they had spotted. Using a couple of pieces of iron bar, Davis was able to remove the dangling handcuff and break the other off Vince. Vince was jubilant, and Davis thought he might kiss him for freeing him from the bracelets. There had been no gunfire that morning, and again it was unusually quiet. After the morning water run, they sat together discussing signaling techniques. They each took turns practicing and setting up the paper signal. No air traffic had been seen in some time. This led them to believe that the fighting was slowing in the area. Around noon, Peter and Davis went to the stream for the midday water run. While there, they talked about the glowing restlessness of the others. If they only had food, it would be different. They could stay out a long time on MREs. At least until secure, safe contact could be made. They realized that as the group became hungrier and became more exhausted, they probably wouldn't be able to hold them together.

Around thirty minutes had passed when the faint but familiar sound of a helicopter approaching from the east could be heard. Davis and Peter scrambled up the stream bank to the others to bring the signaling gear. Everyone sprang to, and some signaled from the quarry, the others signaled from a spot close to the road. The lone helicopter passed over and within a half mile. It just kept on going and disappeared over ridge line without deviation in course. Everyone was devastated and pissed. They kicked the ground. How can this be? How can this happen? What, are they blind? Their anger was cut short, though. Within minutes, the helicopter reappeared. It had made a turn and was coming back in their direction. Still it made no indication that it had it had spotted the Evergreen personnel. They were frantic. They waved a white shirt. They waved the drapes and colored paper, as well as flashing the mirror. The helicopter again disappeared beyond the ridge. The group just stood there in disbelief. Moments later, a flight of five UH-60s appeared out of nowhere and started a wide orbit around the quarry. There were American troops on board. They had seen the Evergreen group.

As they circled just several hundred feet above, one of the helicopters came in and landed on the road. It was the command ship. A lieutenant colonel emerged and asked if they were the people of which he had a handful of identification photos? They were. The LTC indicated that they had been looking for them and asked if everyone was there and accounted for. Davis replied yes except for Bill Farnan and a couple of others that lived on the other side of the base around Veracruz.

He told him that Bill had become separated from the main group two days ago. Davis requested them to look for Bill, and he would show them the general area he was last seen in. The LTC advised Davis that they already had Bill, and he had assisted them in locating the group based on the original plan they had made at the schoolhouse. The commander walked through the group, assessing the situation. He announced that a medivac bird would be there within ten minutes to extract them. The LTC got back in his aircraft and left. He left a squad of well-armed soldiers with the Evergreen group to provide security until they were out of there. Just like clockwork, the medivac came in and landed. They loaded up all nine of the Evergreen air crewmen. The soldiers mounted another helo, and they went airborne. They flew directly to the Joint Casualty Evacuation Center, which was the MASH unit erected on the spot that the CASAs were usually parked on. Upon arrival at the center, they received pajama bottoms, juice, and food. They started attending the wounds on Bill McQuade, Joe Smith, and Vince Cardwell. Jim Miller was given IVs and was in serious condition. He was dehydrated and borderline heat exhaustion. Within the hour, a debrief team had come and gone. The guys gave them information on the locations they were held at, types of weapons, and other useful information concerning the escape. Personnel from the 61st MAG came over for identification purposes. They were then released to the Evergreen operations and maintenance building, which was about a hundred yards up form the C & E Center. They were escorted out and over to their facilities. Terry and Karen Olsen, operations administrator and his wife, were there, as well as Bill Farnan, Doug Beaty, and Jim Hoeber. Jim Ritter, the only flight crew member who wasn't captured that first night, was also there.

During the next several hours, they were given a psychological debriefing by Lieutenant Colonel Greenfield, US Army. The base chaplain came by. The base commander, as well as the Southern Command liaison officer, came and relayed a message from General Thurman. Peter Dickinson passed out hundred-dollar bills for them to purchase clothes and personal items with. The 61st MAG made arrangements with Mrs. Black and the administrative contracting officer for emergency medical evacuation stateside as soon as possible.

That night, eight of the ten flew outbound for Andrews Air Force Base, Maryland. Bill Farnan left for Mexico City, where his wife was residing at their home. For the ten, their Christmas would be in a free land, with their families. The war for them was now over.

The next day, Terry and Karen Olsen left. Ritter caught a flight as well. The CASA 212 program had been raped. They were not operational and would not be an asset till some time later. As for Jim and Doug, they stayed to hold the fort. The CASA project in Panama would need a lot of work to get back to being operational. For now, Casper 212, "the friendly ghost at the end of the runway," was in the pause mode. Within the week, Jim took off for Soto Cano Air Base in Honduras. Evergreen still had aircraft up-country there. Those assets could be relocated to Howard AFB till new personnel arrived. By February, the CASA 212 program was back up and running and fully operational.

About the Author

James W. Hoeber joined the US Air Force when he was twenty years old and served as a jet aircraft mechanic for four years with the 23rd Tactical Fighter Group that was composed of the 74th, 75th and 76th Fighter Squadrons, also known as the "Flying Tigers." Once discharged from the air force, he attended school at Spartan School of Aeronautics in Tulsa, Oklahoma.

After graduating with an associate degree in applied science, he attended Embry-Riddle Aeronautical University at Daytona Beach, Florida, where he studied engineering. During this time at school, he served in the Air National Guard with the 38th CAM Squadron, Tulsa Oklahoma, 149th CAM Squadron, Kelly AFB, San Antonio, Texas, 125th CAM Squadron, Jacksonville, Florida, 172nd CAM Squadron, Jackson, Mississippi, and the 135th Tactical Airlift Group, Baltimore, Maryland. He crewed fighter aircraft such as the F-100, F-4, A7-D, F-102, F-106, F-16 as well as two assignments on C130s.

While attending college, James worked for several fixed base operators in the Daytona Beach area and in 1978 through 1979 worked for Doan Helicopter Services of South Daytona Beach, doing aircraft repair and reclamation on vintage WWII aircraft and conversions of military helicopters to civilian aviation standards.

Later he worked for various Department of Defense contractors such as BASI, Beach Aerospace Inc., GLASCO, Gates Lear Aircraft Service Company and Evergreen Helicopters Inc., CASA PROECT.

From 1984 through 1993, James was assigned continuously on several overseas programs that provided logistics support for aircraft attached to the various commands in Europe, the Mediterranean, North African and Central American theaters, with the exception of a one-year assignment at the naval air facility, Andrew Air Force Base, Washington, DC, in 1988.

James now resides in the Corpus Christi, Texas, area with his wife, Rosa, and son, Andrew. His daughter and her family lives in Boerne Texas.

Photo of author outside residence in Panama

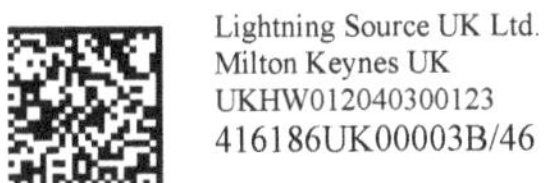

9 781636 921365